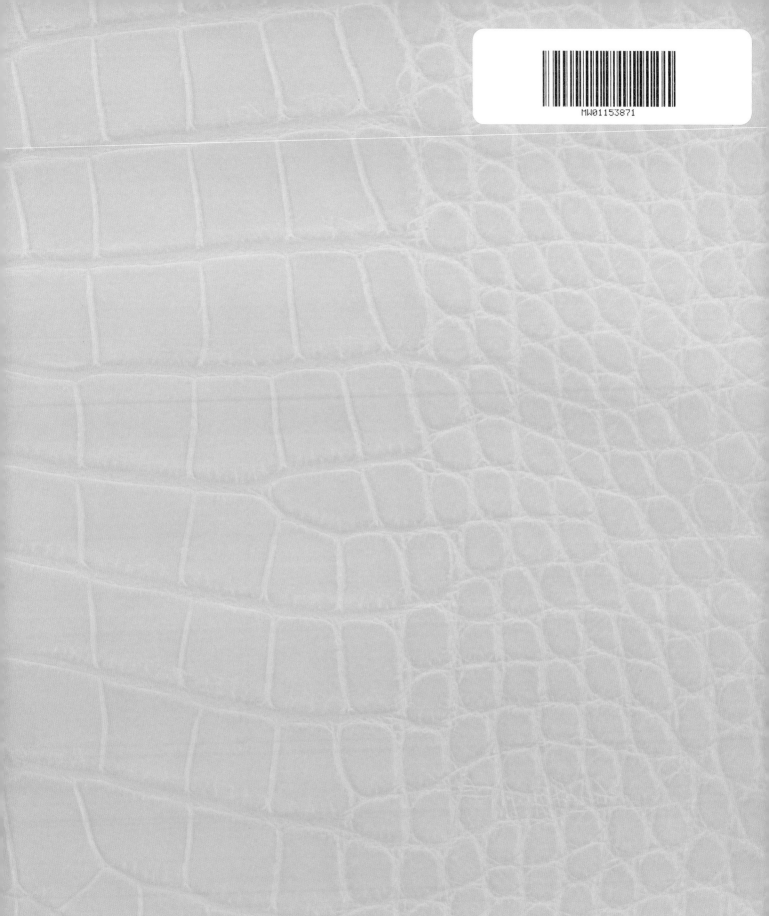

THE ART OF
LEATHER INLAY
AND OVERLAY

A Guide to the Techniques for Top Results

Lisa Sorrell

Schiffer Publishing Ltd

4880 Lower Valley Road • Atglen, PA 19310

Copyright © 2016 by Lisa Sorrell

Library of Congress Control Number: 2016935267

Designed by Molly Shields
Cover design by Brenda McCallum
Type set in FHA Modified Tuscan Roman NCV/Times New Roman
ISBN: 978-0-7643-5121-1
Printed in China

Published by Schiffer Publishing, Ltd.
4880 Lower Valley Road
Atglen, PA 19310
Phone: (610) 593-1777; Fax: (610) 593-2002
E-mail: Info@schifferbooks.com
Web: www.schifferbooks.com

For our complete selection of fine books on this and related subjects, please visit our website at www.schifferbooks.com. You may also write for a free catalog.

Schiffer Publishing's titles are available at special discounts for bulk purchases for sales promotions or premiums. Special editions, including personalized covers, corporate imprints, and excerpts, can be created in large quantities for special needs. For more information, contact the publisher.

We are always looking for people to write books on new and related subjects. If you have an idea for a book, please contact us at proposals@schifferbooks.com.

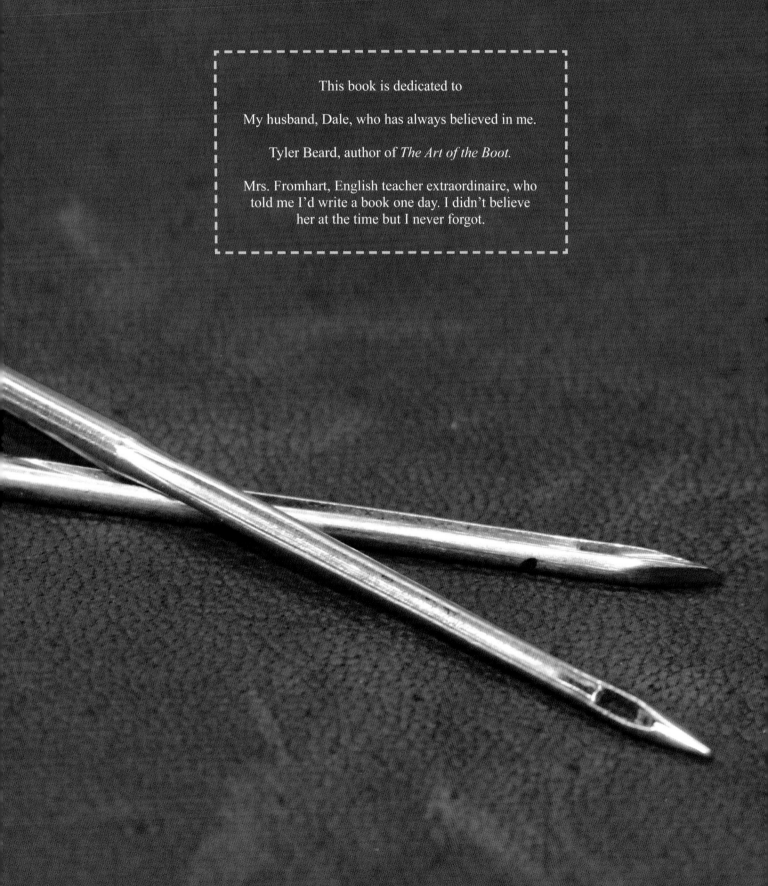

This book is dedicated to

My husband, Dale, who has always believed in me.

Tyler Beard, author of *The Art of the Boot*.

Mrs. Fromhart, English teacher extraordinaire, who
told me I'd write a book one day. I didn't believe
her at the time but I never forgot.

CONTENTS

ACKNOWLEDGMENTS

I would like to acknowledge and gratefully thank:

My parents, Don and Lana Johnson, for giving the gift of a loving and interesting childhood. Special thanks to my dad for teaching me to climb trees, catch snakes, and not be afraid; my mother for teaching me to sew at age twelve, and starting me on the path of a lifelong fascination with making things; and my sister, Lori, for always letting me have the biggest bedroom so I'd have room for my sewing machine.

My two fabulous daughters, Morgan and Paige, who are proud of the fact that their mother wears cowboy boots, and graciously forgave (almost) the times I was late or forgot appointments because I was busy at the studio.

My wonderful father and mother-in-law, Tommy and Myrtle Sorrell, for their support and the many, many times they took care of my girls so that I could attend an event.

Doris and Ralph Halladay, who allowed me to call them "aunt" and "uncle" and always helped out in last-minute emergencies.

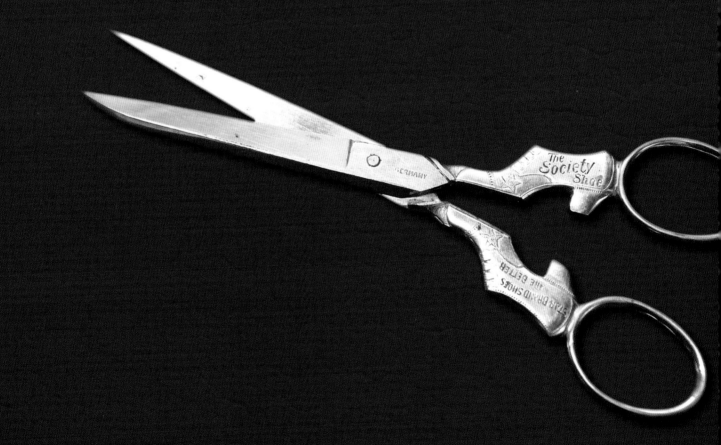

THE HISTORY OF LEATHER INLAY AND OVERLAY

Inlay and overlay are techniques for creating designs with leather. Similar to appliqué in fabric or marquetry in wood, pieces of leather are layered together to create an overall design.

With leather, unlike appliqué or marquetry, each layer must be designed to extend over and/or under the next and the results are stitched into place.

This book details every part of the process of creating inlay and overlay as well as the tools and machinery needed. I've also included information about other decorative leather techniques that can be used in addition to, or in conjunction with, inlay and overlay.

- In appliqué, cut fabric pieces are layered. Since fabric edges will fray, the stitches that hold the pieces in place also serve as a heavy border of thread that binds the edges.
- In marquetry, different shapes or colors of wood are fitted next to each other like a puzzle.

The craft of inlay and overlay wasn't invented by cowboy boot makers; there are stunning examples from many countries and cultures of leather inlay and overlay in vintage clothing and shoes. However, complex inlay and overlay designs are virtually impossible to create solely with machines. As we moved toward a more mechanized society the craft of inlay and overlay became less common within garments and shoes—except in the world of bespoke cowboy boot making.

J. L. Bishop's 1868 *History of American Manufacturers 1608–1860* volume II says, "The manufacture of boots and shoes employs a larger number of persons than any other single branch of American industry, not excepting the cotton manufacture." This was based on data from the 1860 census. He notes that there were 12,487 boot and shoe making establishments nationwide by 1868.

Obviously shoemaking is no longer the number one industry in the United States; to be a shoemaker today is to be an anachronism. Cowboy boot making is the only footwear craft in the United States that's survived relatively intact. Cowboy boot makers are also the ones who have preserved the craft of inlay and overlay. Cowboy boot makers not only preserved the techniques, they took them to the farthest reaches of color and possibility.

Sometime around 1870 regular knee-high boots began evolving into something new and distinct—the American cowboy boot, which was characterized by a more pointed toe and a higher heel. These distinctions might have remained subtle except for the introduction of inlay and overlay. By the 1920s, when the rest of the shoemaking industry began slowly moving to techniques that could be performed in a more cost-effective manner by machines, cowboy boots were beginning to be defined by the use of inlay and overlay using techniques that are impossible to replicate with machinery

alone. While cowboy boots certainly were and are still made in factories, the craft of boot making was never lost to the individual boot maker. There are still many small shops today, sometimes employing a few family members and sometimes operated by just a single maker.

The craft of inlay and overlay has survived within this setting. It's been passed along orally from maker to maker and with a little bit of healthy competition thrown in—each boot maker trying to define his work and outdo his peers—the craft has thrived. However, this history and the various techniques for creating inlay and overlay with leather have never before been documented.

I learned the craft of leather inlay and overlay through working with cowboy boot makers. In 1990 I began working in a boot shop as a "top stitcher." This means I did the decorative work on cowboy boot tops. All of the work was done on an old single-needle Singer sewing machine, the quality of the work entirely dependent on the operator's hand and eye coordination. I spent a year and a half working for that maker before moving on to work independently, producing decorative stitching and inlay and overlay for cowboy boot makers

across the US. Doing the decorative work on cowboy boot tops has traditionally been a woman's job, both in small shops as well as larger factories. Even in modest "one person" shops the boot maker would frequently have a wife who stitched the boot tops, although she was rarely credited for her work and certainly not recognized as being a boot maker.

I later went on to learn the entire craft of cowboy boot making and have owned my own business (www.sorrellcustomboots .com) since 1996. All of the cowboy boots featured in this book were made by me, and they're often used here as examples of the craft of inlay and overlay. However, this is only incidentally a book about cowboy boots.

Until now, the only way to learn leather inlay and overlay has been from a cowboy boot maker, and the expectation has been that these techniques would be used to decorate cowboy boots. My purpose in writing this book is to document the craft of leather inlay and overlay, providing a resource for those who wish to learn—and to also expose this craft to a larger audience outside the world of cowboy boot making. There are many applications other than cowboy boots for leather inlay and overlay, and I look forward to seeing new ways this craft is applied.

HOW I DISCOVERED THE CRAFT

I discovered the art of inlay and overlay through working for Jay Griffith, a legendary cowboy boot maker, who hired me to produce the decorative stitching on boot tops. I had no idea that footwear could be so intricate and colorful. The boots that inspired me to become a boot maker were made by Jay for his wife while they were dating. They were too tight so he tore them down to remake them. In the meantime they married, had three children, and divorced. The boots were never finished, sitting in their uncompleted glory on a shelf in Jay's shop. The endless possibilities of inlay and overlay represented in those cowboy boots were what first attracted me to boot making.

I found the job through an advertisement looking for someone to "stitch boot tops." I had no idea what that was but it sounded like sewing. I called the phone number, and the grumpy old boot maker who answered the phone informed me that sewing leather was nothing like sewing fabric. He allowed me to come in and apply for the job anyway, and I was hired. Jay was right about sewing fabric

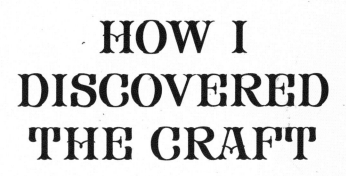

WILL TRAIN 2 people to do fancy stitching on cowboy boot tops. Should have some artistic talent, be able to coordinate colors, and have good hand to eye coordination. Industrial sewing machine experience helpful. Call 282-3824 for interview. A prideful desire to successfully complete a job is a must!!

being different than sewing leather. Fabric will forgive a mistake; leather will not—every hole left by the needle will remain visible.

Working for Jay was a learning experience in many ways; he was an alcoholic with a quick temper and I'd never been around anyone who drank or swore. The sewing machines were different than my fabric machines. The most amazing difference to me was the foot or knee lift, used for raising the presser foot; I'd never seen that feature before. I quickly trained myself to stitch with my left foot so that my right leg was free to operate the presser foot lift. This is not a requirement, but it *is* more efficient. Also, in Jay's opinion scissors were only for fabric so I wasn't allowed to use them, even for snipping threads.

In spite of the steep learning curve and Jay's occasional foul moods, I grew to love both him and working with leather. I was fascinated by the history and tradition of this new craft and amazed at the creative potential of working with leather.

I had grown up in a small community and my mother taught me to sew when I was twelve years old. At age fifteen I had a business sewing ladies' clothing—primarily dresses for women in my church. By the time I found boot making, although I had been sheltered in many ways, I was an experienced seamstress and had been sewing professionally for five years. Boot making appealed to me with its opportunities to wield hammers, handle knives, and operate large and unfamiliar sewing machines.

The opportunity to devote myself to learning inlay, overlay, and decorative stitching was invaluable. It gave me a lasting appreciation for the artistic possibilities in working with leather and the experience to make my visions a reality.

At the time I began working for Jay, he was fulfilling a large order for boots with a single row of decorative stitching on the boot tops. A typical cowboy boot top is composed of four panels—two fronts and two backs. I'd come in to work in the morning to find tall stacks of boot panels waiting to be stitched. He told me he'd raise my pay by 50¢ an hour when I could stitch one row on all four panels in half an hour. I devoted myself to meeting this goal and achieved it within a few weeks. It was a good experience because it taught me to be both fast and accurate.

Decorative stitching on cowboy boots is usually composed of endless curves and my first attempt was not a thing of beauty.

This is the boot that inspired me to become a boot maker. I remember looking at this boot, attempting to memorize every curve and line, and vowing to myself that someday I'd be good enough to make a boot as beautiful.

All of my cowboy boot designs are named after bluegrass and classic country song titles. When I make boots for myself to wear it amuses me to name them after grumpy songs about being tired, broke, and overworked.

"Sixteen Tons"

"Another Day, Another Dollar"

"Up This Hill and Down"

"Working Man Blues"

CHAPTER ONE

TERMS AND TOOLS

INLAY: Creating a design by cutting a shape out of a piece of leather and layering another piece of leather behind the hole.

OVERLAY: Creating a design by cutting a shape out of a piece of leather and laying that shaped piece over another piece of leather.

SKIVING: Thinning the edges of different pieces of leather so that they blend seamlessly into each other when layered.

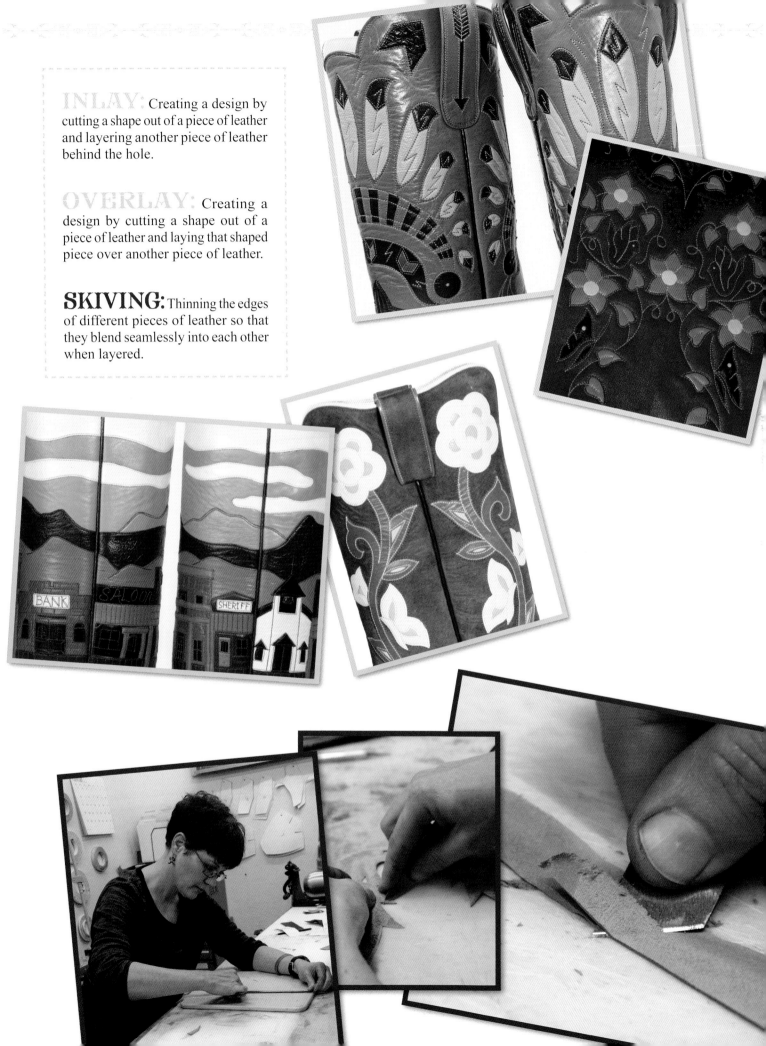

Leather

I could simply say my medium is "leather." But there are many different varieties of leather, and just as many more types of leather styles and finishes. I prefer to work with kangaroo leather and will work with it exclusively in all examples featured in this book unless otherwise noted, as it is thin but very also strong. The kangaroo leather I use is chrome-tanned, which means tanned with chromium salts, allowing for a larger range of colors and brighter hues.

Leather has two sides. The grain side is the finished surface of the leather. This is the top side, the side from which the hair has been removed, and it's the strongest and best side. The other side is called the flesh side. The grain side is usually smooth and shiny and the flesh side is fuzzy, similar to suede or nubuck. The back side of finished leather is called rough-out. I occasionally use rough-out as a decorative technique or if I simply like the color of the back side of the leather better than the finished side. Regarding the back side of the leather as a new and different color option can be helpful since color options can be limited.

It's difficult to find kangaroo leather in the US in a wide variety of colors. I'm always searching for sources for kangaroo leather and I buy unusual colors whenever I find them, even if it's not a color I need at the moment. Kidskin is readily available in a rainbow of colors, but it's usually slightly heavier and never as supple. It's also harder to skive and dulls the knife quicker. As part of my quest for more and better leather and color options I've become a dealer for a kangaroo tannery in Australia and I also sell kidskin in metallic colors.

Leather should never be folded; it must be rolled to avoid wrinkling and cracking the finish. I have racks that hold multiple rows of PVC pipe and I store the leather inside the pipes. I use thin-walled 4-inch PVC pipe. It comes in 10-foot lengths and I cut these into thirds, so each pipe is a little longer than 3 feet. This is the perfect size for storing kangaroo and kid skins. The only exception to the "no folding" rule is ostrich. Ostrich leather can be folded just like fabric.

Rubber cement is a glue that provides a temporary bond; it's only used for applications where the leather will be stitched into place later. Rubber cement is typically solvent based and has a strong chemical smell.

When applied to the glossy, smooth side of leather it can also create a thin, clear, sticky coating that's easy to remove. This sticky layer will hold temporary pattern markings so they don't disappear as you work.

While there are certain situations where the regular solvent-based rubber cement works best, I try to avoid solvent-based glues as much as possible. I prefer to use the Aquilim line of glues by Renia because they're water-based, non-toxic, and have no hazardous fumes. After years of using solvent-based glues I was becoming sensitive to the fumes so I was searching for substitutes. I found the Renia Aquilim glues on a trip to Germany, and I took samples home and tried them. They performed much better than I anticipated and it was with great excitement I emailed Renia to ask where I could purchase the glue. On being told that the answer was "nowhere in the United States" due to no dealer being here, I volunteered to stock the glues and sell them. Being able to cut down on hazardous fumes in my own shop and help others do the same has been very satisfying.

There's also an Aquilim contact cement, which is a permanent bond. This is the Aquilim 315. A contact cement is often necessary to complete leather projects, but it's not used for creating inlay and overlay.

Aquilim SG is a re-positionable water-based rubber cement; it should be thinly applied to one surface and allowed to dry thoroughly. After it dries it can be bonded to another surface, pulled off, and stuck down again multiple times.

Aquilim GL is a water-based rubber cement; it should be applied to one surface and then bonded while still wet.

These are the tools needed to create leather inlay and overlay. A sewing machine is also a necessity; sewing machines for leather are covered in chapter 13.

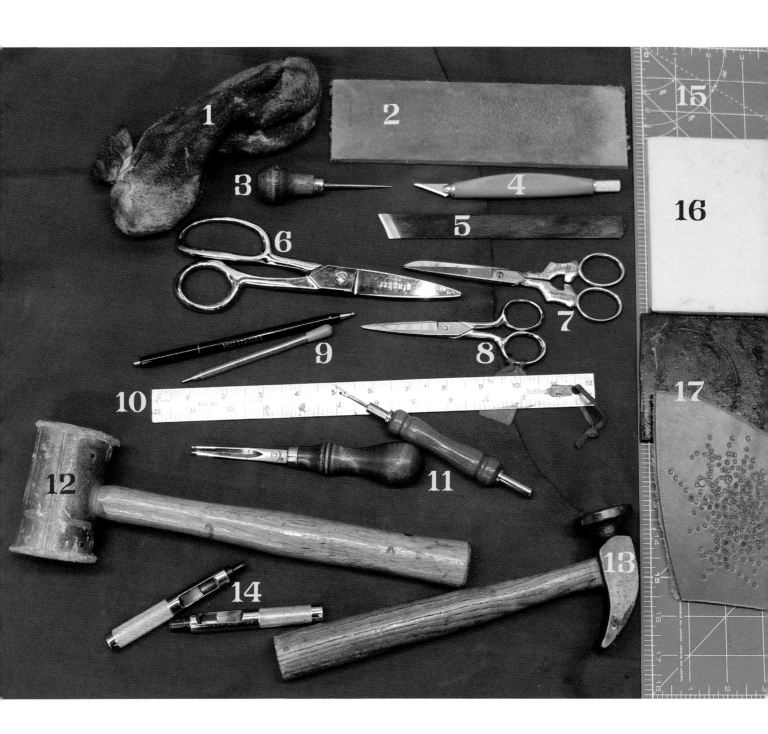

1. **Powder bag:** thick sock filled with baby powder or blue builder's chalk, and used to transfer designs to leather. A baby powder sock is used most frequently, but it's also necessary to have a sock with blue builder's chalk for marking on light-colored leathers.

2. **Strop:** Piece of heavy leather rubbed with polishing compound, for buffing a knife edge to keep it sharp.

3. **Scratch awl:** Small pointed awl. These are handy for pulling a loop of thread to the back side of the project, lifting a small piece of leather that's stuck in the wrong place, and making small marks in poster board to guide the placement of patterning lines. I keep one of these on every sewing machine table and at every work bench.

4. **X-Acto knife:** Craft knife with a small pencil-sized handle and pointed, replaceable blade.

5. **Skiving knife:** Specialty knife for thinning the leather edge.

6. **Scissors:** Normal-sized pair that fits your hand comfortably. They're the most versatile and I use them often. These are *only* used for leather, never paper.

7. **Paper scissors:** I always keep one pair of scissors at my bench that can be used for paper.

8. **Small scissors:** Small pair with a sharp point, for precision work. Again, these are *only* used for leather, never paper.

9. **Silver pen:** Specialty marking pen with silver ink, designed specifically for making marks on leather that can be removed later. I do not use regular silver gel pens as I find that they do not remove easily from leather.

10. **Metal ruler:** Not just for measuring, this is also a guide for cutting straight lines. This is why it must be metal, so the knife blade will run alongside it without cutting into the edge.

11. **Edger:** For trimming excess leather from behind a beaded edge. The Common Edger is a traditional leather working tool, but a fabric seam ripper will also work. This tool is pictured and demonstrated in chapter 11, Beading.

12. **Mallet:** Rawhide or plastic mallet. This is the tool to use for hitting metal punches.

13. **Pattern Hammer:** A hammer with a large, gently rounded face. It's used to lightly compress leather layers prior to stitching. ***It is never used to hit a metal punch, as this will mar the hammer face.***

14. **Punches:** Hole punches for creating small precise holes in leather. These are most commonly small circles but other shapes can be used as well.

15. **Cutting surface:** A self-healing cutting surface that will not dull a knife blade. A plastic cutting board will work; so will a fabric cutting mat.

16. **Marble or glass:** A slick surface that won't cause the knife to catch or drag is essential for skiving.

17. **Punch mat:** A thick piece of rubber or heavy leather, placed under a hole punch prior to punching. (Using a hole punch directly on the hard cutting surface will break the punch edges and destroy the tool.)

Pro tip: Sand a smooth side on tool handles to keep them from rolling off your bench every time you lay them down.

CHAPTER TWO
INLAY AND OVERLAY

An inlay is created by layering a piece of leather behind a hole cut into a larger piece of leather. For instance, if I had a large piece of leather and I cut a butterfly-shaped hole into it, then put a different colored piece of leather behind that hole, I would have created an inlaid butterfly.

An overlay is also created by layering pieces of leather together, but the desired design shape is cut and laid on top of another piece of leather. If I wanted to make an overlaid flower, I'd cut a flower shape out of a piece of leather and then place the cut flower on top of another piece of leather.

The art of inlay and overlay has been preserved and has flourished within the craft of cowboy boot making, with designs invariably drawing their inspiration from nature; eagles, butterflies, birds, leaves, and flowers were all common motifs. These themes are still in use today and I return to them often for design inspiration. Again, leather inlay and overlay is not limited to cowboy boots; many projects can be created and enhanced with these techniques. The potential for inspiration is endless.

Inlaid butterfly, bluebird, flower, and leaves.

Overlaid flower and stem with leaves.

It's also possible to mix inlays and overlays. Designs can increase in detail and intricacy through:

- Layering an overlay on top of another overlay
- Creating an inlay within an overlay
- Adding an overlay within an inlay
- Creating an inlay within an inlay

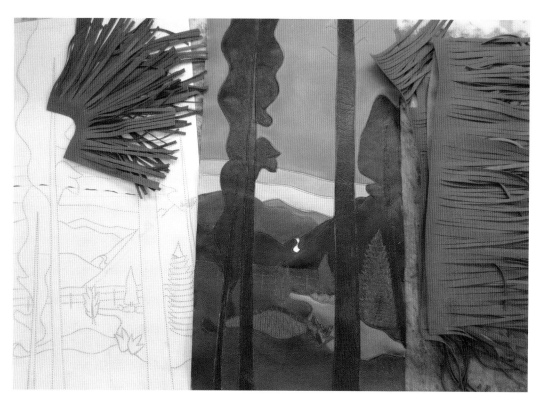

This is the pattern and partially completed design for a pillow I created after a trip to Montana. This was the view out my window each morning.

I titled the completed pillow "Wild Montana Skies."

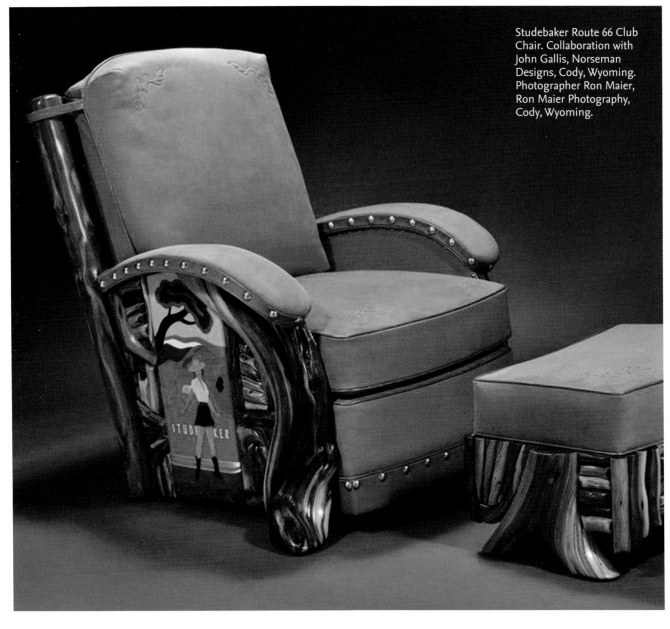

Studebaker Route 66 Club
Chair. Collaboration with
John Gallis, Norseman
Designs, Cody, Wyoming.
Photographer Ron Maier,
Ron Maier Photography,
Cody, Wyoming.

An important part of planning a project is determining if it will be inlaid or overlaid. Sometimes this simply comes down to personal preference, but often there's a specific reason for choosing one or the other. Because inlay and overlay are created with separate pieces of leather, each distinct piece must be sewn into place—glue alone will not hold the leather indefinitely.

A design with very narrow elements such as skinny letters or flower stems would generally need to be inlaid, as the roller wheel of the sewing machine will tend to either "fall off" or "shift" a strip of leather that's too narrow. Inlay is also a good option for designs with small elements that don't touch each other. Since the stitching goes around the outside of inlaid pieces, it can be used to connect separate parts of the design and make them all work together.

This small flag represents the narrowest possible inlay. The red stripes are very slim overlay pieces and the white is the inlay behind them. A close look will reveal the difficulties I had keeping the roller wheel (and therefore the stitching) on the red stripes.

As an overlay, holding these small leaves in place while they were being stitched would have been difficult. An inlay, sewing around them, ties the design together and adds visual interest.

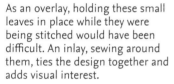

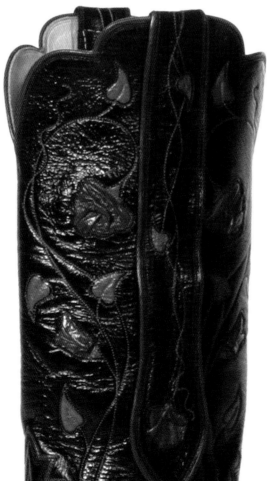

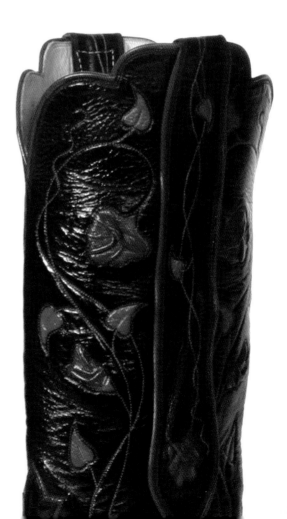

Overlay works well for larger design elements. A large piece of leather can be glued in place and won't move as it's being stitched. Overlay is also a better choice for any type of latticework design such as the connected stems and leaves in the following designs.

There are many components to successfully creating leather inlay and overlay. Each edge must be skived or thinned so there are no bumps and ridges where pieces join. It's essential to choose a proper skiving knife, keep it sharp, and know how to use it.

Each piece must be stitched into place, so it's necessary to have a sewing machine. This machine must be set up for sewing leather and be maintained properly.

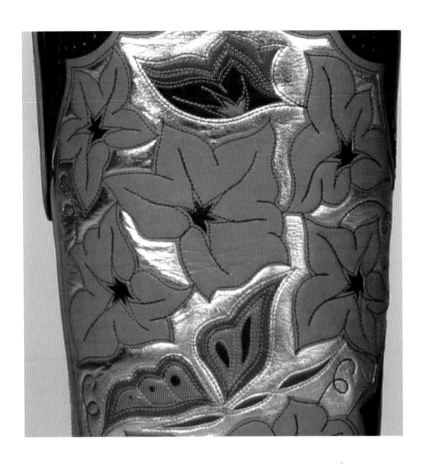

Inlay and overlay can be used together also. The large green overlaid leaves are all cut out of one piece of leather that's laid over the gold, while the butterfly and flower are inlaid into the gold.

Both the leaves and flowers are overlaid. An attempt to inlay a design that covers this much area would result in a web of leather too fragile to stitch into place.

This design works exceptionally well as an overlay. The design is cut into the gray leather and then the entire piece is laid over purple leather. Notice how the gray leather is all one piece—sometimes connected only by a small flower petal tip.

CHAPTER THREE

STITCHING

It's not enough to cut, skive, and layer the leather in order to create an overall design that works well—each piece must also be stitched into place. It's possible to create beautiful images and art with leather, but the medium does have its limitations. There's no way to blend one color into another as you can with paint; each bit of leather remains separate and distinct. Sewing the leather does more than just secure different layers together; it adds another element to the work and this must be anticipated as you plan your work.

Done properly, the lines of stitching can add a suggestion of light and shadow, depth, and visual interest to the work. Stitch lines add small details that are impossible to produce with inlay and overlay, and stitching is also the only way to add a degree of light and shadow to the work. In the following images I've defined the petals of a flower and the wings of a bird with stitching. Before I sewed the leather, the bird was simply a boring bird-shaped blob, but the stitching lent coherence, personality, and movement.

I used the same technique for this pin-up cowgirl. She's supposed to be curvaceous, but without an ability to use light and shadow there's no way to convey that with leather inlay and overlay alone. By stitching a plaid design onto her shirt, lines are created that follow the curves of her body, and she suddenly develops the intended figure.

Stitching can alter the dimensions of inlay and overlay work. In order to "sew in" an inlay, it is stitched around the hole cut for it. The stitched line of thread causes the design to visually appear bigger. If I inlaid a square that was ½" by ½" and stitched all around that square at ¹⁄₁₆" from the edge, the square would then visually appear to be ⅝" by ⅝", because the stitching becomes a part of the overall impression of the image. The only way to lessen this effect is to match the thread color of the stitching to the color of the leather that's being stitched.

This is a large overlay floral design. Notice how the center flower and the two bottommost flowers have a stem that extends under the flower. This small stem becomes an inlay at the tip because it extends *under* another piece.

All of the overlay pieces are in place, but without stitching, the design looks flat and featureless.

Stitching adds visual interest and breaks up the monotony of large pieces.

Overlay pieces are sewn to another piece of leather, with the stitching on the overlay piece itself. This can produce the reverse effect of inlay, making the overlay piece appear to shrink. Of course, the color of the thread can also be matched with the overlay to lessen this effect.

Additional rows of stitching can also be layered next to each other. This can be done to reinforce an edge or to more strongly define the stitch lines. Each additional row of stitching should follow as closely to the first as possible, with about a needle's width between the rows. Always use the smallest needle and finest thread possible—using a larger needle leaves bigger holes and requires more space between the rows of stitching.

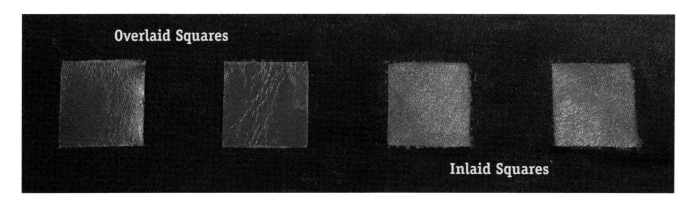

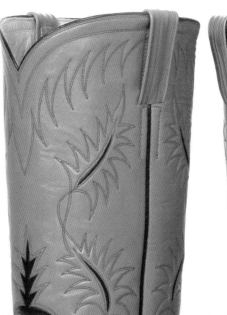

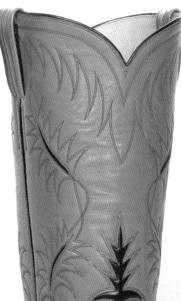

The Art of Leather Inlay and Overlay

Multiple rows of stitching can be used to enhance inlay or overlay or it can stand alone to form an intricate design without inlay and overlay. When sewing multiple rows of stitching it's necessary to consider spacing in regard to not only the previous row, but also the first row. Ten rows of stitching should uniformly be about ½" wide throughout the entire design; it should not be ¼" wide in some areas and 1" wide in other areas.

You can judge the precision of the stitching by looking at the back of a project. Without the distraction of colors it's easy to focus on the accuracy of the stitch lines.

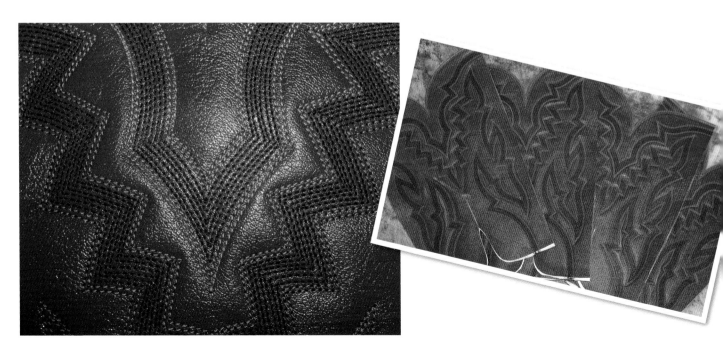

If a design is symmetrical, you have points that are supposed to mirror each other. Since these areas are reverse images of each other, you'll be approaching one point from the bottom and one from the top as you're stitching.

For example, let's say you're stitching a maple leaf with its distinctive three-pointed shape. If you begin sewing at the stem, you'll approach the first of the three points from the underside, stitching toward the top of the leaf. You'll continue on around the second leaf point, which is in the center, then start toward the third and final leaf point. This third leaf point is a mirror image of the first leaf point, but now you're approaching it from the top of the leaf, and sewing back toward the stem. This opposite approach to mirrored design elements can yield points that angle in different directions unless special care is taken.

The solution is drawing contour lines. Using a silver leather-marking pen, extend each point in the desired direction. If the points are on each side of a centerline it's easy to make certain that they point directly at each other. When you sew, these contour lines will indicate exactly where to pivot. Taking a few moments to draw contour lines before stitching will give your project a pleasing symmetry.

A variation of multiple stitching is fill stitching. With this type of decorative sewing each design element is outlined with one row of stitching. Rows are then added next to the original first row, working inward until the space is completely filled. This technique looks incredibly difficult and inspires much admiration, but in reality it's the easiest version of multiple row stitching. Because there are so many sewing lines to distract the eye, small imperfections are less noticeable.

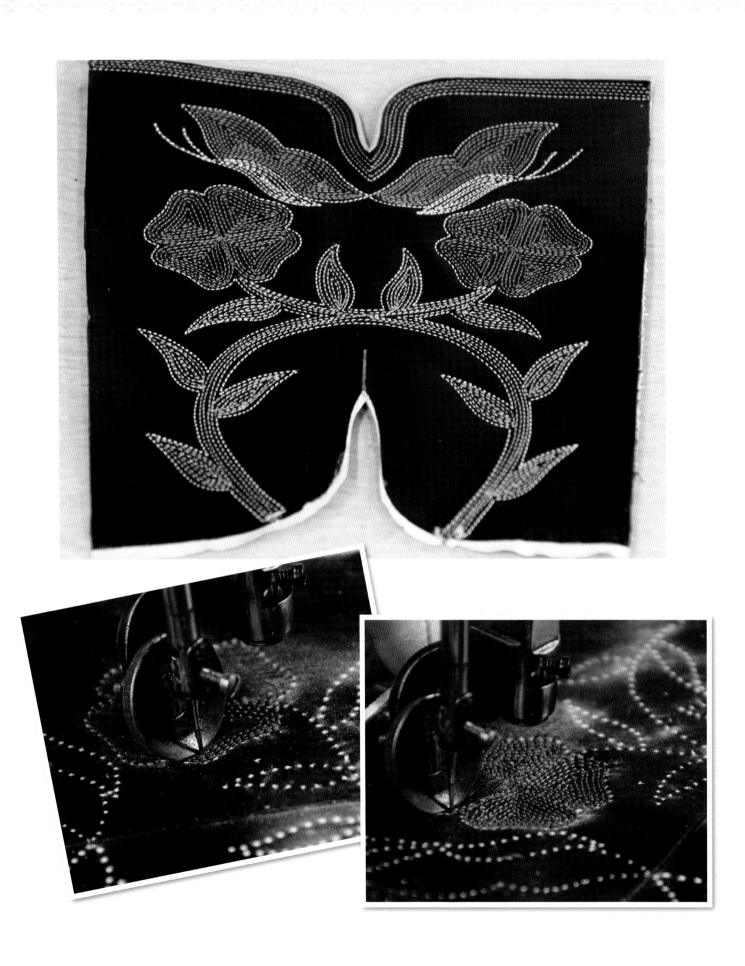

CHAPTER FOUR

PATTERNING

I cannot stress enough the importance of patterning, both for achieving optimal work the first time, and to ensure that you can produce identical results when later attempting to recreate a project. I create a pattern piece for every single piece of leather I cut. Obviously I need a pattern for the primary design, but I also have pattern pieces for each inlay backing piece, as well as each overlay shape.

I prefer using white poster board for patterns. I like white because my drawings show up well, and I choose a matte finish because I find it more difficult to sketch on a coated finish. I enjoy the feel of a pencil in my hand, so I draw my designs freehand directly onto the paper most of the time. I sometimes use carbon paper to transfer designs or parts of designs but computers, graphic design programs, and printers can be used also.

When the design is drawn onto the poster board it has to be finalized in a way that makes it permanent and allows it to be transferred to the leather. I do this by stitching the design directly onto the poster board on my sewing machine with no thread in the needle. A size 14 or 16 needle works best, so that the holes will be large enough to allow pattern transfer. Once the design is stitched into the poster board you'll have a series of small holes that define the design.

Always put a scrap piece of poster board under the design when you stitch it. This supports your pattern piece so the holes in the design will be clean and open.

For inlay and overlay work, the perforated pattern can be used to mark the design onto more poster board to create pattern pieces for the various components of the inlay and overlay. When it's time to transfer the design to the leather, the poster board is positioned over the leather and the powder bag (a sock full of baby powder) is rubbed over the design. The pattern can be marked onto the leather multiple times to refresh the lines needed for cutting and stitching.

The pattern pieces for inlay should always be about ¼" bigger than the hole that they're filling, to provide enough material to sew together, as well as allowing enough room to skive down the edge so that it can't be seen from the top of the design. The rule for skiving and stitching is that you always want to be sewing through a full, or almost full, thickness of leather. If an inlay piece is about ¼" bigger than the hole, when you stitch the design the sewing will go through the area right where the skiving begins. This way you'll be sewing through the strong,

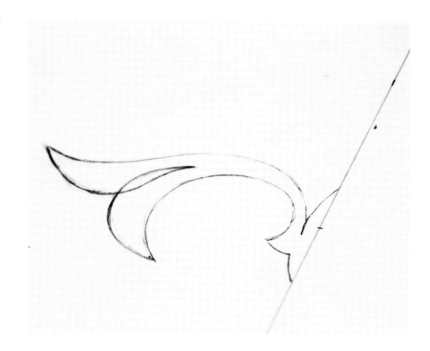

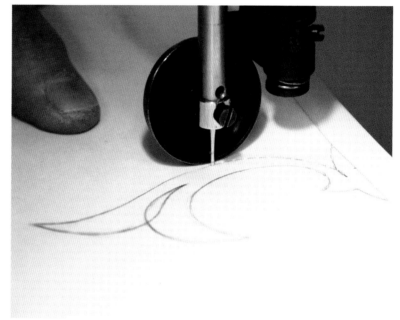

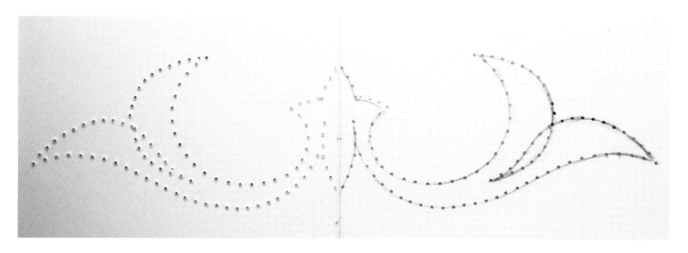

Remember, if a design is symmetrical you can draw half, fold it in half on the centerline, and stitch it.

When you open the design each half will match perfectly.

Sometimes when design elements are very small, they're unclear when defined by needle holes. In these instances I cut them out of the poster board rather than stitching them with the needle.

full thickness of leather, but it will immediately begin feathering out to a thin and invisible skive.

Inlay pieces should be soft approximations of the hole that they're filling. The inlay piece for an inlaid sunflower wouldn't have the sharp points of a sunflower, but would loosely be a flower shape with gently rounded points. If the sunflower were small the inlay piece could just be a circle with no petals defined at all. The outside dimension of the circle should be ¼" bigger than the tip of each petal.

When inlay patterns are done precisely, there are very few areas that are two full thicknesses of leather. The wide skive on the piece that's underneath should begin exactly where the narrow skive on the top piece starts. Because the skive underneath is wider than the narrow skive above, there's a small area that's slightly more than one full thickness of leather. This area is so narrow and slight, though, that it's not visible to the eye or apparent to the touch. The overall feel of perfectly skived inlay work is that of one continuous thickness of leather.

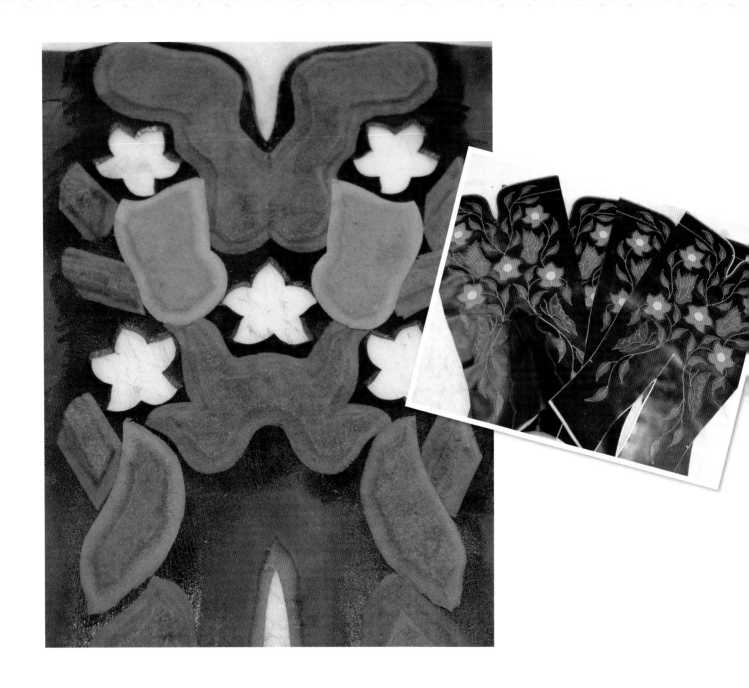

Narrow skive   Wide skive

It pays to be meticulous with details when creating a pattern. I always mark each pattern piece with information about it. I write the color of leather, note the number of those pattern pieces I need, and circle that number. If the design is symmetrical, with design elements that mirror each other, I make a note of that information as well. If I needed eight of the same inlay piece, but four needed to face one direction and four the opposite direction, I'd write "4<" and "4>." In this instance I'm using the "greater than" and "less than" symbols (> and <) to remind me that the pattern piece should be reversed when I mark it onto the leather. These symbols indicate that I should cut four with the pattern writing side up and four with the pattern writing side down to reverse the image. I also note which part of the design the inlay piece is, such as "Butterfly Wing" or "Top Feather."

To make working with large pieces of leather easier, create patterns for overlay pieces that are close to the size and shape of the final overlay piece. Cutting out an approximate shape for an overlay pattern lets you work with a piece of leather that's the correct size instead of manipulating the whole piece of leather as you try to cut out a precise shape. Cut out a shape of poster board that's big enough to hold the overlay design piece with very little excess. Use that poster board pattern to mark out the pieces of leather needed, then mark the design onto the leather and cut out the exact shape with an X-Acto knife.

Sometimes with smaller overlay design shapes I'll cut the exact shape out of poster board, trace around it with a silver pen onto the leather, then cut it out with scissors or an X-Acto knife. It just depends on my mood!

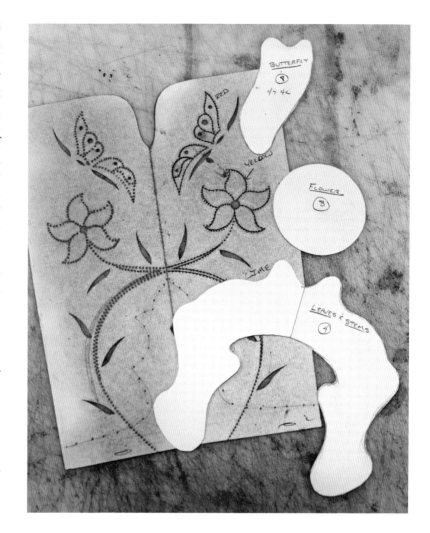

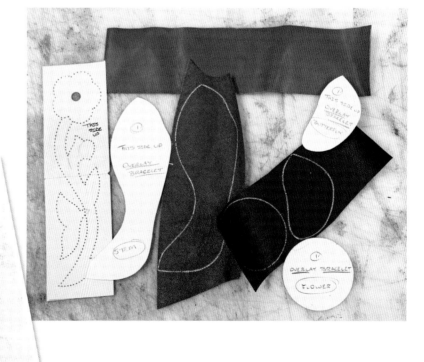

The best tool for marking the pattern onto poster board or dark-colored leather is the powder bag, a sock filled with baby powder. If the leather is either white or light in color, baby powder won't show. Because of this I also always keep a smaller sock with blue builder's chalk in it for use with lighter colors, as well as for transferring a design to white poster board.

In order to transfer the pattern to the leather, put a thin coat of rubber cement or water-based rubber cement substitute on the smooth side of the leather. This light coat of cement will hold the baby powder dots in place as you're working, and it will be removed later. This step *can* be skipped but if you work without the glue base you'll need to be very careful to avoid touching the baby powder dots, as the slightest brush of your finger will obliterate them. It's very important to remember that the glue in this step should be applied as thinly as possible. If you're using solvent-based rubber cement, work quickly to spread the glue out thinly and evenly.

If you're using the water-based Aquilim GL, ***thin it with water***. Aquilim GL at full strength can alter the sheen of finished leather. I keep a small jar on my bench that contains a solution of half Aquilim GL and half water. I never use this to glue anything permanently together, only to make the leather tacky so it will hold the pattern markings.

Allow the cement to dry completely to form a thin, slightly sticky layer on top of the leather. Position the poster board pattern on the leather and then rub the powder bag over the pattern. The baby powder will come through the sock and fall through the holes in the poster board, transferring the design in a series of small white dots that are "glued" to the leather when the poster board is carefully removed.

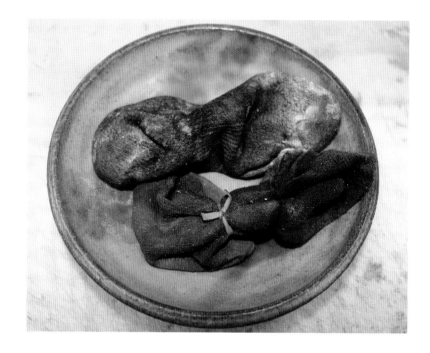

Sometimes it's necessary to *gently* bounce the powder bag against the poster board so the powder will fall through better. Don't violently bounce the powder bag. This can cause so much powder to fall through the holes that the design is obscured by the sheer volume of powder.

Use the chalk markings as guides for cutting or stitching the leather.

Never put a thin coat of rubber cement on suede or rough-out leather. The cement cannot be removed; it will bond with the leather fibers and never come off. For rough-out you simply have to mark the design on with powder (no glue!) and try be careful as you're cutting and stitching so the marks remain until you're finished. The good news is that baby powder sticks to rough-out a little better than to smooth leather, so you're less likely to accidentally brush it off as you're working.

Another handy tool for making marks on leather is a silver pen. These are specially formulated for marking on leather and the marks will usually come off cleanly. Notice I said "usually" because there are occasional exceptions. Silver ink is difficult to remove from rough-out, and if it's allowed to sit on the surface of any leather too long it will dry

If you choose to apply a thin coat of glue to the leather to hold the pattern dots you'll need to rub off the dried glue with a gum eraser when the project is completed. A gum eraser is basically just a big block of dried rubber cement, so it sticks to the dried layer of glue and pulls it off.

in place and can't be removed. It can be wiped off after two or three days but if allowed to stay for two to three weeks it may become permanent.

Be careful if using a silver pen on leather with a matte or unfinished appearance; it works best on a glazed finish. I wouldn't put a thin coat of rubber cement on leather just for silver pen markings, but if there is already cement on the leather it makes it easier to remove the silver ink. The ink markings will be on the cement instead of the leather and will come off when you rub away the cement.

I like to use the silver pen for tracing around inlay pieces—the parts that go behind the main body of the design. Since I cut a poster board pattern for each design element it's easy to position them on the leather and trace around them. While fine accuracy on most inlay pieces isn't too important, because they sit behind a precisely shaped hole, there are times when a leather piece must be cut *exactly* the right shape. Sometimes, for very small, intricate inlays, each piece must be perfect. For this reason it's helpful to develop the ability to cut precisely in the middle of a silver line or exactly inside or outside of the line.

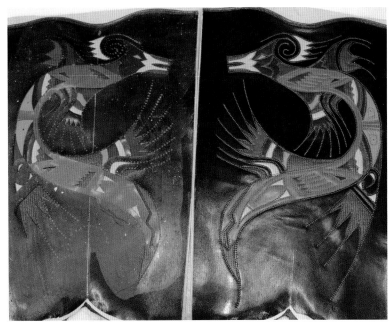

CHAPTER FIVE

SKIVING

As I mentioned in the introduction, leather inlay and overlay is similar to marquetry in wood or to appliqué in fabric, where different pieces are layered together to form a pattern or design. In marquetry the wood pieces are butted up against each other, each piece fitting exactly against the next. For appliqué the different pieces of fabric extend over and under each other and the raw edges are finished with stitching to prevent fraying.

Layering leather can create bumps and ridges. This uneven texture can detract from the visual quality of the intended design by giving the eye something to focus on that distracts from the design. An essential component of leather inlay and overlay, in order to produce a consistent surface, is skiving.

Skiving is a leather-working term that refers to thinning the edge of a piece of leather, going from full thickness to extremely thin at the edge. When an inlay or overlay piece is skived along the edges, a bump or ridge cannot be felt, and more importantly, cannot be seen.

There are two types of skiving—wide skiving and narrow skiving. These terms refer to the width of the skive, or angle, that's sliced away. An inlay piece that goes behind another piece of leather must seamlessly blend into the background. A wide skive, which tapers gradually from full thickness to as thin as possible, allows a layer placed behind another piece of leather to disappear without any trace of an edge. A piece of leather that extends over another layer is narrow skived. It also needs to blend at the edge, but because each piece must be stitched into place, this edge will be sewn. A wide skive would create an edge that's too fragile to hold a stitch, while a narrow skive allows the edge to blend but leaves it heavy enough to hold a stitch.

Skiving is always performed on the opposite side of the leather that will be seen in the finished design. As a rule the grain, or shiny, finished side of the leather is visible and the flesh, or fuzzy side, is hidden underneath. Skiving is usually performed on the flesh or rough side of the leather.

The obvious exception is if the project calls for rough-out leather—the flesh or fuzzy side of the leather—to be used as part of the finished design. Then it would need to be skived from the grain side to preserve the flesh or rough-out side. I often opt for rough-out leather as a design feature, either because I prefer the slightly different shade offered by the back side of the leather, or to add another dimension of texture to the piece.

To thin, or skive, the edge of a piece of leather requires an extremely sharp knife. It's important to hold the knife properly. To get the proper skiving angle you must adjust the angle of the knife. Holding the knife at a shallow angle, so that it's almost flat against the skiving surface, will result in a wide skive. Holding the knife at a steep angle will result in a narrow skive.

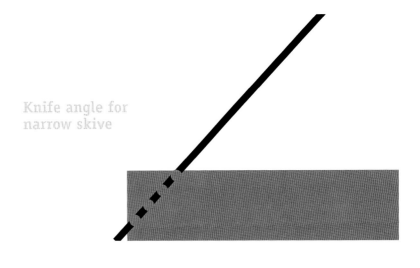

Knife angle for narrow skive

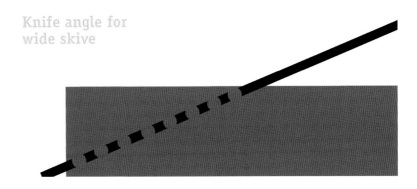

Knife angle for wide skive

An experienced skiver can make this process look incredibly easy but it takes a lot of practice to master; when I teach a class I like to start my students with a morning of doing nothing but practicing skiving on long strips of leather. Ideally I'd love to have them practice skiving for about two solid weeks, but one morning seems to be the limit of both their patience and the time we can realistically allot. No one has ever perfected skiving in one morning, however. Practically speaking, I'd expect a student or apprentice to be a good and versatile skiver after about six months.

- Skiving is difficult to master and requires hours and hours of practice.
- It's impossible to create fine leather goods without skiving.

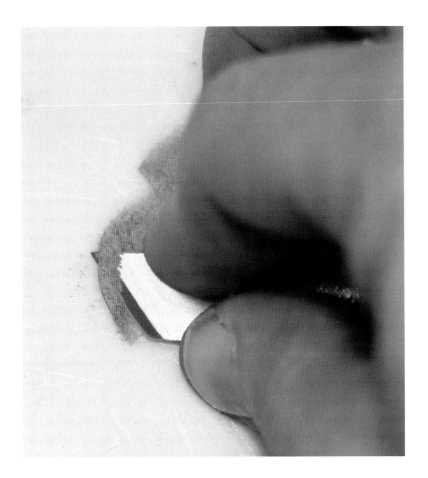

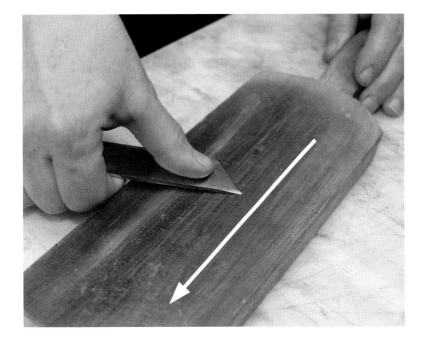

Practice, practice, and practice. It will get easier.

I also can't emphasize enough the importance of a razor-sharp knife to skiving. There are many sources for advice on sharpening a knife and devices for making it easier, so I'm not going to approach that subject here. Find a system that works for you and keep your knife sharp!

One thing I will suggest for keeping a knife sharp is buffing it regularly on a leather strop coated with a polishing compound. Before you use the knife, after you finish using it, and at very regular intervals throughout, rub the knife blade firmly and quickly backwards across the leather strop. Pull the knife toward you across the strop with the blade away from you; don't push the knife blade into the leather. The knife should be held at a very slight angle—almost flat—to keep from rounding the blade edge and dulling it.

Before we begin exploring various types of skiving knives and different angles for skiving, note that machines exist for skiving. The most common is called a bell knife skiver. The blade is a circle, kind of like a bowl or a bell. As you feed leather through the skiver the blade spins and skives the leather edge, and it can be adjusted to create different angles and widths of skive.

A bell knife skiver is wonderful for long straight edges, adequate for gently curved edges, and absolutely useless for intricate inlay and overlay, as it can't reach into tiny corners and curves. It would be dangerous and scary to use for small pieces, and it can only skive outside edges, not complex holes cut into leather for inlay. To create intricate designs with smooth, imperceptible edges it's essential to learn to skive by hand.

There are many different types of skiving knives. I have opinions about which skiving knives work best, and over time you will develop your own preferences. The main thing is to find a knife that works well for you. This must also be a knife that you're able to keep sharp.

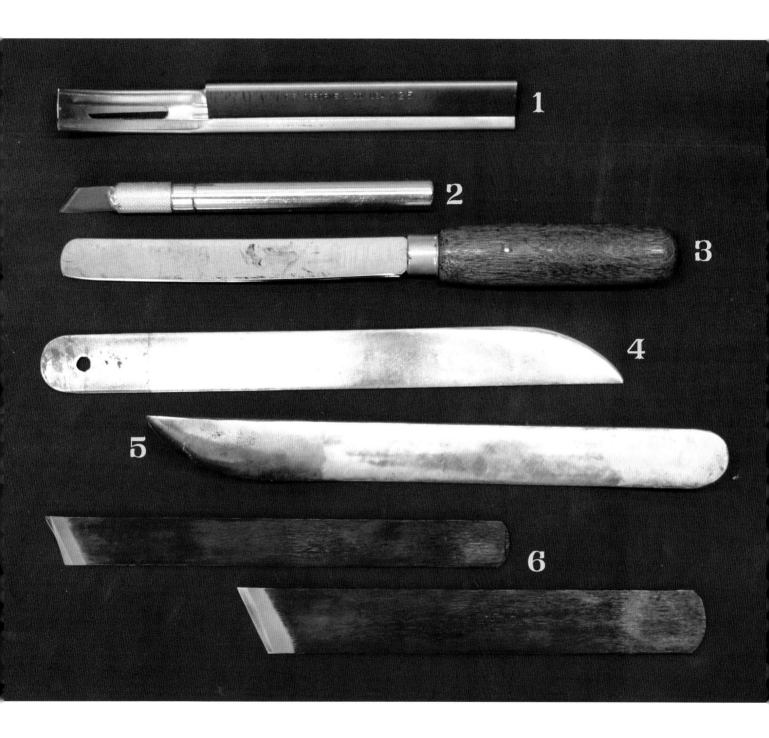

1. This knife is called a scife. It uses a replaceable razor blade which it bends into a curve to assist in cutting off the leather edge at an angle. If you own one of these my advice is to throw it away and buy a real knife.

2. This is a heavy-duty X-Acto knife with an L blade. These are the knives I give my students in classes. They're adequate for narrow skives but they don't work very well on heavy leather or for very wide skives. I use them for classes because they're an easy and inexpensive introduction to skiving. Best of all, these blades are disposable and replaceable. I always demonstrate and encourage my students to try a real knife, but using disposable blades in a class is an easy way to make sure everyone's knife is sharp at all times.

3. The blade of this knife is long and flexible; to skive you push the blade flat against the skiving surface and hold the handle up, creating a curve in the blade. This is the type of knife I used when learning to skive at my first job in a boot shop. I never mastered getting *all* of the long blade sharp at the same time and I dreaded and hated skiving. This was the only type of knife I saw boot makers using and I thought it was the only knife for skiving. I was so relieved and happy to discover, years later, that there were other options.

4. This knife is a flat piece of steel and the cutting edge is a curve. It works well, but keep in mind the sharpening process. I personally find sharpening a curved blade to be more difficult than sharpening a straight blade.

5. On this knife, not only is the cutting edge a curve, the whole knife itself is a curved piece of steel. This type of knife is quite common in Europe. I find it incredibly difficult to sharpen and in my opinion it works best for splitting. Splitting is thinning the entire surface of the leather from the back, reducing a heavy piece of leather to a thinner piece. However, I know shoemakers who are quite skilled at both sharpening and using this type of knife for skiving.

6. These are the knives I use in my shop. The absence of a thick handle is crucial here. Without a handle you can adjust the angle of the cut; add a handle and you'll be unable decrease the angle sufficiently to create a long skive. These are always the knives you'll see me using in demonstrations for this book, in my YouTube videos, and in my classes. I have different varieties that I've bought over the years, but I have them made especially for me now (and I also sell them through my web page). I use both a ¾" and a 1" wide blade for different skiving applications.

CHAPTER SIX

SKIVING TECHNIQUES

Some applications call for a very narrow skive and some call for a wider skive. Leather inlay and overlay is created with different pieces of leather that are layered together, and each piece of leather must be stitched into place. A narrow skive is used for any edge that's on top and will be stitched. A wide skive is used for any edge that extends under another piece of leather. Students often ask me, "Does this piece need to be narrow skived or wide skived?" I respond with another question: "Does it go over or under? If it goes over it's a narrow skive; if it goes under it's a wide skive."

There must be tension on the leather as you skive so the edge doesn't curl away from you as you're skiving. Use the knife with one hand and hold the leather firmly to the skiving surface with the other, but make sure you always hold the leather behind the area where you are cutting. *Never hold the leather with your forefinger and thumb and skive between them so that your knife is cutting toward your thumb.* If the knife slips, you'll slice into your thumb.

When you stitch the leather you want to be stitching through full or almost full thickness of leather. If you make a wide skive that's very long and thin and then stitch at the edge of it, the leather won't be strong enough to hold the stitch and it will tear.

The width of a skive, especially a wide skive, is influenced by how thick the leather is. Kangaroo and kidskin are typically about 0.08 to 1 mm in thickness. These are lighter-weight leathers, perfect for creating the multiple layers of inlay and overlay without adding weight and bulk.

Leather inlay projects should always be lined. This sandwiches the inlay pieces between the main piece and the lining, so the inlay edges that are underneath can't curl or roll. Overlay projects don't necessarily have to be lined.

The weight of lining leather I choose depends on the finished project. I would use 0.08 to 1 mm kangaroo lining leather to add as little weight as possible to a project. I use a heavier 1.5 to 2 mm lining leather for boot tops because I don't want the boot top to fall over limply. I also like the way a heavier lining leather can add a pleasing hint of "puffiness" to a completed design.

When skiving you should be able to see the very point of the knife tip at all times. With a short, non-flexible blade like I use only the tip should be visible; if too much of the knife extends out past the leather edge it will affect the angle of the skive. On the other hand, if the knife tip is not visible and doesn't extend out past the leather edge, the skive will either not be cut off completely or it will slice additional leather from the edge.

LEATHER THICKNESS CHART

MM	IRON	OUNCE	FRACTION
0.4	0.75	1	1/64
0.8	1.50	2	1/32
1.2	2.25	3	3/64
1.6	3.00	4	1/16
2.0	3.75	5	5/64
2.4	4.50	6	3/32
2.8	5.25	7	7/64
3.2	6.00	8	1/8
3.6	6.75	9	9/64
4.0	7.50	10	5/32
4.4	8.25	11	11/64
4.8	9.00	12	3/16
5.2	9.75	13	13/64
5.6	10.50	14	7/32
6.0	11.25	15	15/64
6.4	12.00	16	1/4
6.8	12.75	17	17/64
7.2	13.50	18	9/32

The angle of the blade in relationship to the leather edge being skived is very important; the blade edge should ***not*** be perpendicular to the leather edge. This is the most common mistake that beginning skivers make and it's a very hard habit to break. Attempting to skive with the blade perpendicular to the leather edge will result in pulling and stretching the leather, and you will end up cutting out chunks rather than smooth skives. The reason this method doesn't work is because you're attempting to use the entire blade edge at once (like a woodworking chisel would be used).

The proper method is to hold the blade at an angle next to the leather edge. This means that the back edge of the blade will begin cutting before the front point. The knife should slice along the edge, beginning the skive at the thickest point with the back end of the blade. The front tip of the blade follows, continuing to slice the leather as it creates the skive.

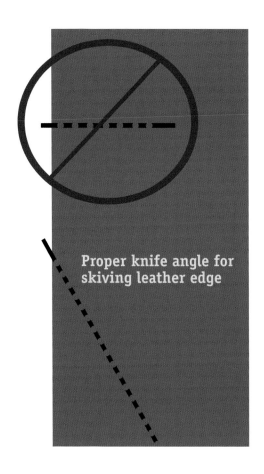

Proper knife angle for skiving leather edge

The width of a skive can be influenced by the thickness of the leather, but for kangaroo leather a narrow skive should be about ⅛" wide. The blade should slice through the leather edge at a steep angle, entering the leather at about ⅛" from the edge to create a narrow skive. A narrow skive is the easiest one to learn and to master.

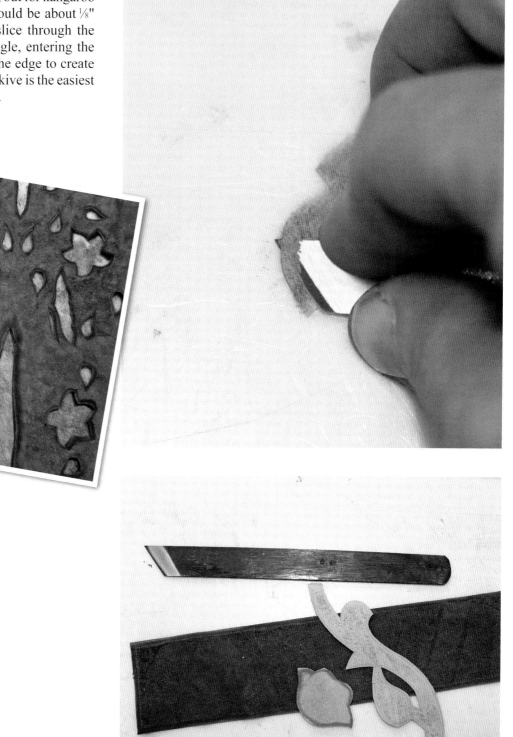

Wide Skiving

A wide skive is the hardest one to learn and to do it well requires a real knife that's absolutely sharp. The width of a wide skive depends on the width of the leather. For 5- to 6-oz. leather I cut a skive that's about ⅝" wide using the 1" skiving knife. For thin kangaroo leather, though, a wide skive will only be about ¼" wide. The ¾" knife is wide enough to work well for both narrow and wide skives on kangaroo leather.

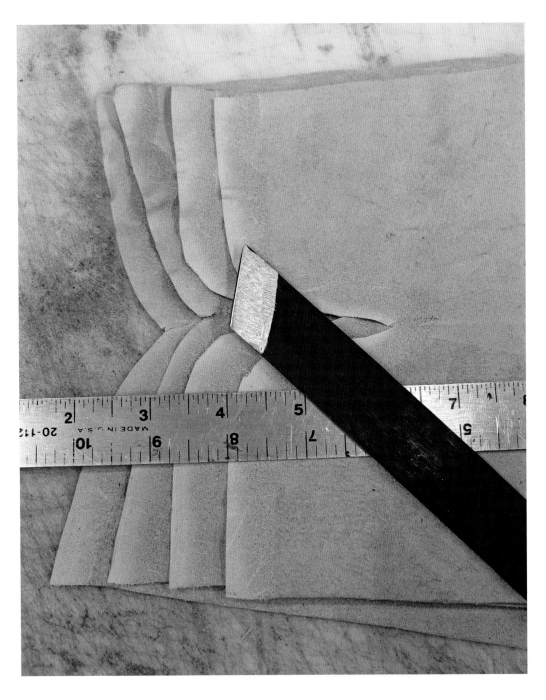

Fuzzing

This is a term that I made up to describe a common attempt at skiving. I often see students try to skive by repeatedly shaving off a thin layer of leather. I don't even have to see them doing this to know what they're doing; I can look at their work surface and know. Fuzzing creates little fuzzes of leather, but doesn't remove enough leather to thin the edge and enhance the work.

A proper skive results in a long strip of skived leather. An experience skiver can cut an even 18" long skive off an 18" strip of leather. If each skive blends seamlessly into the next, though, it really doesn't matter if you're doing one long skive or short bursts of skiving. Just make sure you're actually skiving and not fuzzing.

Push Skiving versus Pull Skiving

Whether you're narrow or wide skiving, there are two options for the direction of the cut. You can ***pull skive*** (pull the knife toward yourself) or ***push skive*** (push the knife away from you). Some leather workers are quite vehement about which of these is "right" but I'm only interested in results. I've had students who are more comfortable and better at push skiving and students who are more comfortable and better at pull skiving. I frequently tell students, "I don't care if you do it with your teeth, just give me a clean skive." Obviously using your teeth to skive is not possible but the point is that each person should use the technique that yields the best results for them—but remember to never cut with your thumb in front of the knife!

I prefer pull skiving, and if you watch my videos, this is the technique that I'll use most often. There's no danger in pulling toward yourself *if your knife is sharp*. A sharp knife will glide cleanly through the leather and is easy to control. A dull knife will drag and jump—it's the dull knives that cut you!

The important thing about holding the knife, no matter if you're pull or push skiving, is that your fingers are not curled under the knife. Don't clasp the knife with your fingers wrapped around the handle. Instead, you should grip the sides of the knife. If your hand is clutching the knife with fingers underneath the handle, you won't be able to adjust the angle as you skive. Your knuckles and the bulk of your fingers will prevent adjusting the angle of the blade as needed.

Whichever method you choose there's just one small problem—how to start on a corner or a piece of leather that extends out

Pull skiving: For pull skiving the proper technique is to lay your fingers lightly on the blade with just the tips around the edge of the knife. Your thumb should rest on top of the knife near the edge.

Push skiving: For push skiving hold the knife with your thumb under your fingers and against the edge of the knife, and lay your index and middle fingers on the top of the knife near the cutting edge.

into a narrow tip. No matter which way you're going you can't start at a corner of thin leather and begin skiving. It will wrinkle up and, even if you're able to begin skiving, you'll cut uneven chunks. The solution to this is to start with the alternate method to the one you prefer. For instance, I prefer pull skiving—this is the method that's most comfortable for me and I like to use it most. So I push skive off all my corners, then I come back and finish the rest of the edge by pull skiving.

Another area where both pull and push skiving is required is inside corners—where a shape angles into a V. Here it's necessary to pull skive down into the V from one direction and then push skive down into the V from the other direction. The goal is to skive exactly to the center from both directions. The knife cuts will meet in the center of the V and the skived leather can be neatly lifted out.

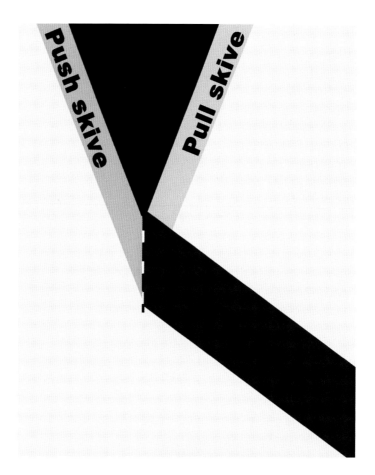

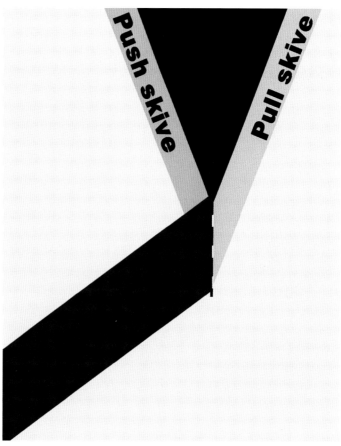

Keeping the work surface clean is crucial. If you leave small bits of skiving on your work surface, one will eventually get under a piece of leather you're skiving. As you skive, this scrap will create a small bump and you'll end up skiving a chunk out of your leather. If this is an inlay piece that will go behind another piece of leather, then it's not such a big deal, but if it's an overlay piece, you've just taken a chunk out of a visible edge.

As you skive, make a habit of brushing the skiving surface clean of leather fragments and pieces.

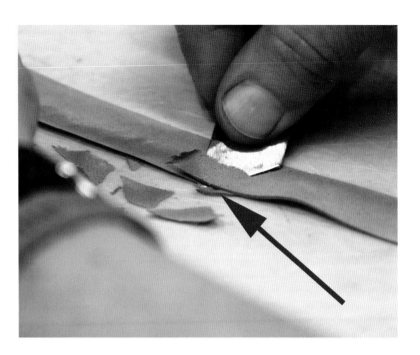

I know some leather workers who skive on a piece of curved glass such as an antique car window or a (very) large glass bottle. Their reasoning is that the curve will encourage these bits of leather to fall off naturally instead of needing to be brushed off continually. I find that kangaroo leather has a lot of static cling. It sticks to my skiving surface, it clings to my skiving knife, it often has to be scraped off the floor, and when I sweep it into the dustpan the static causes it to spontaneously leap back out. It's for this reason that I'm dubious a curved surface would be helpful for skiving kangaroo, so I use a flat piece of marble or glass.

One of the things that surprised me the most about working in a boot shop was that detritus from working was casually brushed off onto the floor. It is the job of an apprentice or the lowliest employee to keep the floor swept clean. I still remember my annoyance at watching someone brush trash onto the floor I'd just finished sweeping. However, this really is the most efficient way of dealing with the debris created from cutting and working with leather. Keep your work surface clean by continually brushing scraps onto the floor and sweep up regularly.

CHAPTER SEVEN

CREATING LEATHER INLAY

An inlaid design is created by cutting the desired shape out of the main body of leather and then layering another piece of leather behind. I use an X-Acto knife to cut out the holes that form my inlaid design, as I prefer the thin pencil-like handle and the maneuverability of the pointed narrow blade.

I refer to the piece of leather that's layered in behind the main body as the "inlay piece." I prefer to use scissors to cut out the inlay pieces that will go behind. Because the edges of an inlay piece won't be seen (as they are underneath another layer), inlay pieces have softly defined edges and absolute accuracy usually isn't essential. The inlay piece must have a wide skive so that the edges won't be visible, creating a bump or a shadow from the finished side of the piece. Using a narrow skive around an inlay piece would leave a ridge outlining its dimensions that shows through the leather on the finished side.

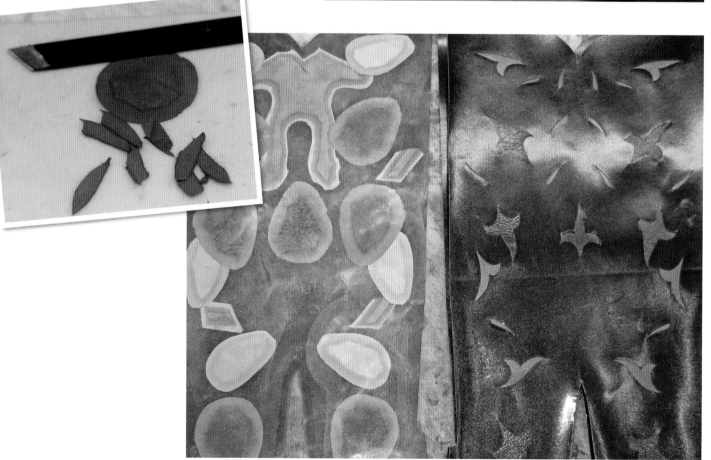

The edges of the hole cut out of the main body for the inlay must be skived also, to produce a smooth transition from one color to another. These edges require a narrow skive so when the leather is stitched you'll be sewing through full or almost full thickness of leather. Using a wide skive around the hole cut for an inlay piece will result in a weak edge. With wear or tension the leather is likely to tear along the stitching.

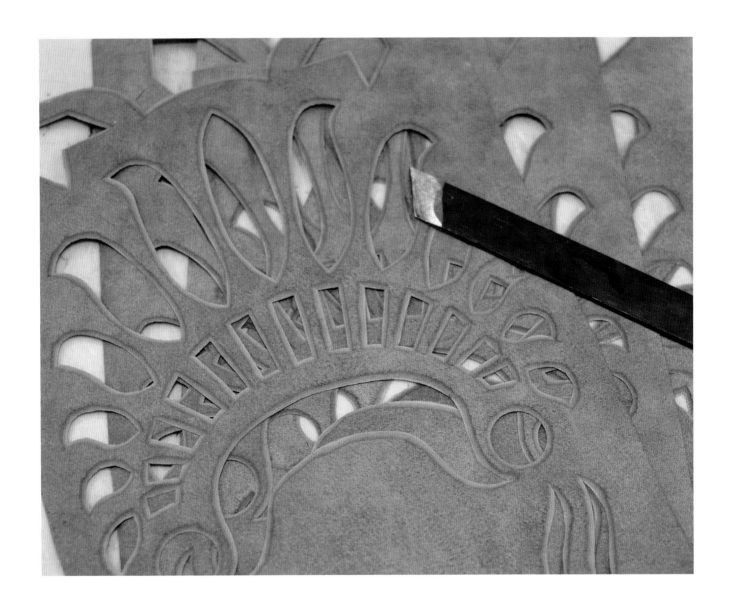

To make the poster board inlay patterns take the primary pattern (the one with the design stitched with no thread in the needle) and lay it over blank poster board. Using the powder bag with builder's (blue) chalk in it, mark the pattern onto the blank poster board. Create a poster board piece for each element of the inlaid design.

Work with one element of the design at a time to create the separate inlay pattern pieces; don't try to mark the entire pattern on at once. Mark each individual element onto the poster board and cut it to the shape required.

If inlay holes are close together you'll need to think about the order you'll be placing them into the design. An inlay piece can't be so big that it extends into another element of the design, but once a hole is filled the inlay pieces next to it can overlap previously positioned pieces.

When you create an inlay design, you're cutting a specially shaped hole out of the main body of the leather and then filling that hole with a different color. The shapes that are cut out of the main body of the leather can be thrown away, but they can also be put to use on another project. I've been told that in the 1930s and '40s, when leather was scarce, boot makers would save the cut-out pieces; if they made an inlaid butterfly boot top, instead of throwing away the cut-out butterfly shape they'd make a second boot top that featured an overlaid butterfly made from the first boot's inlay cut-out piece. This would certainly be an efficient use of leather.

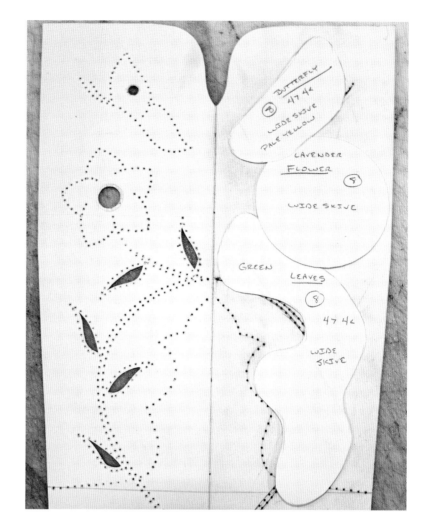

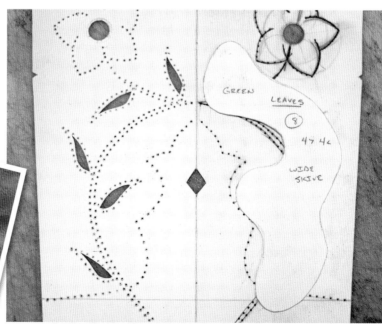

If there are small elements close together (like a spray of leaves) then sometimes it's better to make one piece to cover the entire spray.

A second suggestion for using the cut-out inlay pieces is a technique called "putting the plugs back in." To do this, create the inlaid design as normal. Save each inlay shape as you cut it out. When you've finished cutting out and assembling the entire inlaid design, narrow skive around each cut-out shape. Mark the entire design onto the leather again from the *back*, and then cement the inlay pieces back into place on the back of the design.

In other words, the cut-out pieces should be behind the inlay pieces of leather that were previously layered in. Adding the cut-out pieces pushes the inlay pieces outward, and this creates another layer of dimension and interest.

Sometimes it's desirable to add another layer of inlay within an inlaid element. A bluebird might need a small hole punched out and inlaid to create an eye, a butterfly can have additional elements inlaid into its wings, or a flower could have a different colored center added. Using multiple layers of inlay is a great way to break up large design elements and bring in new colors. Be sure to add these additional layers prior to replacing the plug.

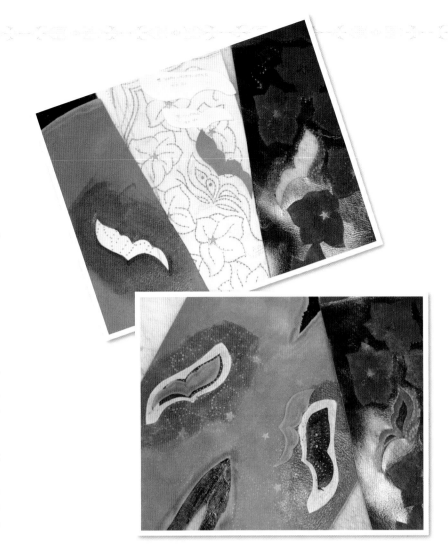

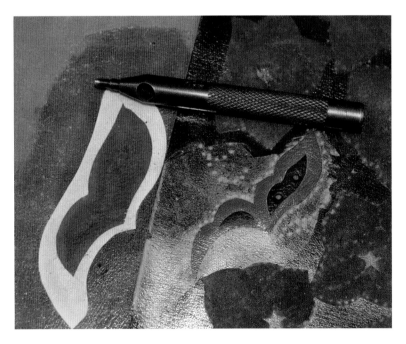

Don't try to cut tiny little patterns for very small design elements. There is a simple way to fill in small inlay holes such as flower centers or small leaves. Cut a long strip of leather that's a bit wider than the hole, skive the strip along both long edges with a wide skive, and cut off short pieces to fill in small holes.

Working from the back of the skived strip, skive the narrow end of the strip. Move up the strip a little and slice/skive off a small piece of the strip. Continue to move up the strip, slicing/skiving off bits as you go. One end of the diamond will be skived from the front side and one from the back side. The important thing is that the resulting piece will be skived on all edges. Use these small diamond or square-shaped pieces to fill in inlay holes that are too small to have specials patterns made for them.

Later on in the section on edge finishes we'll talk about "beading." Since this is how the leather is prepared to make beading, I call the long strip of leather a beading strip.

CHAPTER EIGHT

CREATING LEATHER OVERLAY

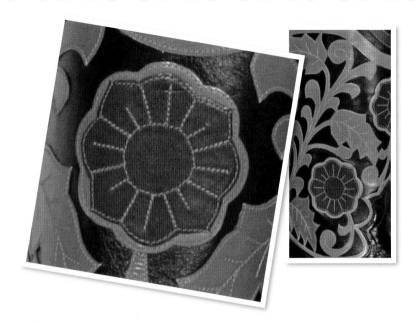

verlay is created by laying specially cut shapes on top of another piece of leather to form a design. Because the overlay pieces are on the top and will be stitched through right next to their edges, overlay pieces should be narrow skived. I enjoy doing overlay and I find it to be faster than inlay. With inlay, the cut-out hole needs to be narrow skived *and* the inlay piece that goes behind the hole needs to be wide skived. Overlay pieces only require narrow skiving and then they're ready.

Overlay works best for larger design elements. Each piece of leather has to be stitched into place—it's easy to punch a hole into a flower and create an inlaid center, but it would be difficult to sew a tiny little overlay circle onto the center of a flower. Overlay also works well for design elements that cover large areas of leather without interruption.

The background color for an overlay is important because it needs to enhance and draw attention to the overlay. The one exception I make to relying on kangaroo leather is a preference for metallic kidskin as a background color. Kidskin comes in a variety of metallic colors and I like the way a metallic background shines and draws attention to the overlay work.

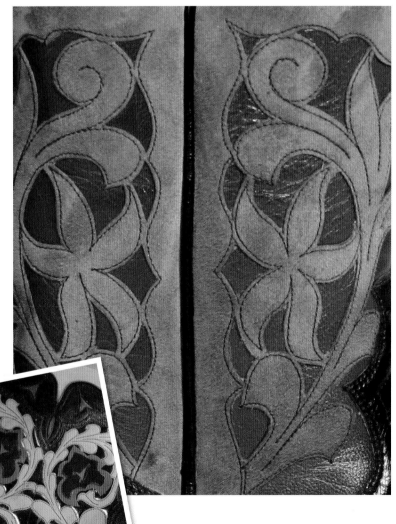

The Art of Leather Inlay and Overlay

As with inlay, I also create poster board patterns for each piece of overlay.

For a complex overlay shape I apply a thin coat of rubber cement to the leather and use powder to transfer the design. If the overlay pieces are simple I often cut them exactly out of poster board and then, using a silver pen, trace around the poster board pieces onto the leather. When I use this method I don't have to worry about losing powder markings as I handle the work and I also don't have to rub glue off the leather after I'm finished.

For larger elements, make a pattern that's a rough outline of the pattern element, and big enough to accommodate the overlaid design. Lay this pattern onto the leather and cut out an appropriately sized piece for the overlay element needed. This eliminates the need to mark a complex design onto a large piece of leather and then deal with a lot of excess material when cutting out intricate shapes.

Before I began this method of cutting out pattern pieces for each overlay element, I laid the design itself onto the leather and rubbed the powder bag over it to mark the pattern onto the leather. I would often accidentally get too close to the edge and lose part of my design, or position the pattern too far from the edge and waste leather. It was much more difficult to ensure that I was using the leather in the most efficient way possible.

In addition to securing the leather pieces together, using stitching is important as a decorative element for overlay. Because overlay pieces are large they tend to look bland and shapeless before they're stitched.

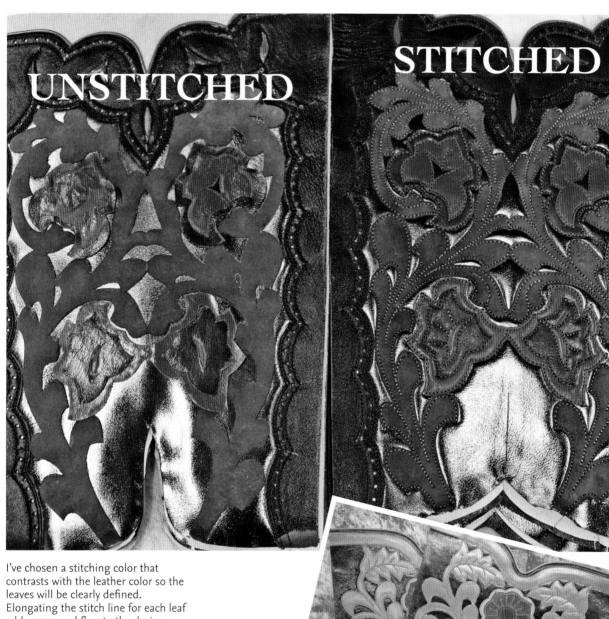

UNSTITCHED

STITCHED

I've chosen a stitching color that contrasts with the leather color so the leaves will be clearly defined. Elongating the stitch line for each leaf adds grace and flow to the design.

For multiple layers of overlay, such as this golden yellow and red flower, I often remove a background layer behind the overlay. In this example the golden yellow flower has a wide-skived interior hole cut out of the center that's slightly smaller than the red flower. This creates the illusion of a double overlay with none of the bulkiness.

Complex designs require both inlay and overlay techniques, so thinking the design through and patterning it correctly are crucial. Every color in a design is a separate piece of leather and each of those pieces must either go over or under its neighbor. With intricate designs a single piece of leather in the overall design may require a wide skive in one area and a narrow skive in another.

Remember: If the leather goes *over* another piece, it needs a narrow skive. If it goes *under* another piece, it needs a wide skive.

In the following example, the eagle's wings are formed from multiple pieces of leather. The topmost feather extends under the cut-out shape of the eagle, so this area of the feather has a wide skive. The second feather extends underneath the first, which means that the bottom edge of the first feather becomes an overlay—so it needs a narrow skive.

Before I started on the design I did two important things. Firstly, I spent some time thinking about and planning how I would create it. I decided that for the feathers, the bottom edge of each would be narrow skived and the top edges would be wide skived. When I began putting the pieces together I started with the top feather and worked my way down the wing.

Secondly, I made creating a precise pattern a top priority. Look carefully at all of the information I have written on each feather's poster board pattern. I numbered each feather so I would know the order of the pieces. There are eleven feathers—#1 is the top feather, #2 is the second feather from the top, and so on to #11, the bottom feather. The circled number is the total number that I need of that inlay piece.

For this project, I was creating a boot top with two front panels and two back panels, which means I inlaid a total of four eagles, each with two wings. Eleven feathers formed each wing and I needed eight of each feather. Because the wings are mirror images of each other I needed four sets of feather pieces for the wings on the right side and four sets of

feather pieces for the wings on the left side. The number 4 and the < and > symbols tell me to cut four with the pattern facing up and four with the pattern facing down.

Finally, I noted which color of leather each inlay piece should be.

To show where narrow skiving is needed and where wide skiving is necessary, I've drawn lines along the edges of the poster board patterns. I don't normally include these markings on my designs, but they illustrate for this example where each type of skiving is needed. A line very close to the edge means a narrow skive and a line farther from the edge indicates a wide skive.

I don't consider time spent making patterns to be time wasted; I often invest quite a bit of time into thinking about the best way to pattern a design and then creating individual pattern pieces for each component of the design. However, once I get started cutting leather I can have an incredibly intricate design completed very quickly, because I made notes about how many pieces to cut and where and how to skive those pieces. All of the elements of the design go into their places without hesitation.

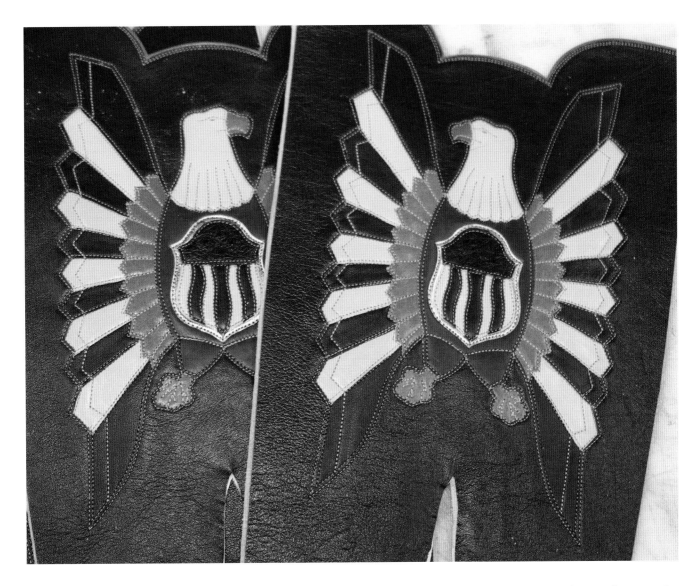

CHAPTER NINE

CUTTING THE LEATHER

owever intricate or simple your design, all of the pieces will need to be cut out by hand. I prefer using an X-Acto knife for cutting leather because the handle is small and it's comfortable for me to hold. I buy the better-quality stainless steel blades and sharpen them rather than throwing each blade away when it gets dull. They're easy to sharpen and respond well to being buffed on a leather strop.

I hold the X-Acto knife with my thumb, forefinger, and middle finger, extending my little finger out and resting it firmly on the leather/cutting surface. My little finger is always resting firmly on the cutting surface as I work, providing support and stability as I move the knife and cut the leather. I never hold the knife up in the air with only the tip of the knife touching the leather—it leaves the knife unsupported and the cut is more likely to wander.

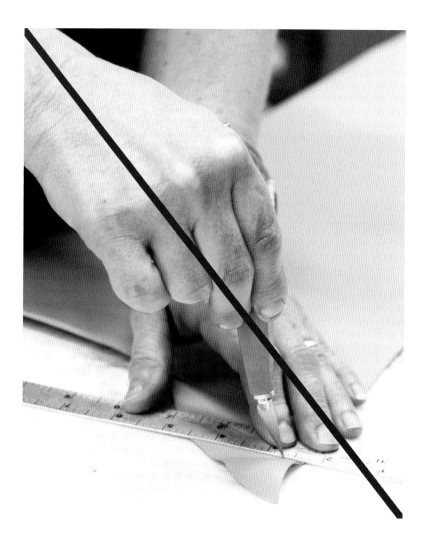

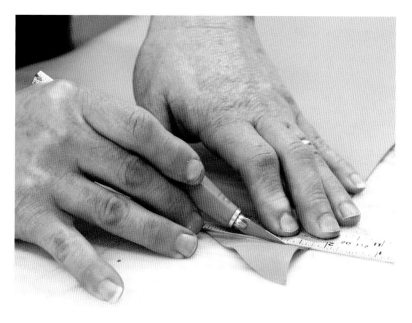

Cutting small curves is a particular challenge. A curve, large or small, should always have a nice smooth shape and never have corners; small curves are especially difficult. I've learned to master the challenge of cutting small curves by using the forefinger of my other hand as a guide for the knife when cutting curves. While this sounds like it could be dangerous, when done properly there's no risk. As I cut around a curve I brace the flat side of the knife blade against my fingernail. This steadies the blade as I cut and allows me to cut evenly and smoothly. Because the flat of the blade is against my fingernail I'm never cutting toward my finger, so I can't cut myself.

To create precise straight lines, use a metal ruler. Position the ruler on the edge to be cut and draw the knife down alongside the ruler. Hold the ruler firmly to the leather with the thumb and forefinger of the opposite hand next to where you're cutting with the knife, and don't allow the ruler to shift position. When cutting a very long straight edge it will be necessary to reposition your fingers as you cut so that the ruler stays tight against the leather as you use the knife.

Do make sure that your thumb or forefinger does not extend out past the edge of the ruler. I was teaching a class one time and I began by giving my students a stern lecture about knife safety. Within five minutes I was cutting a straight edge, talking, and not paying attention, and sliced off the edge of my thumb because it was hanging over the side of the ruler. I attempted to convince them that I'd done it on purpose to demonstrate the awful effects of not using a knife properly, but I don't think they believed me.

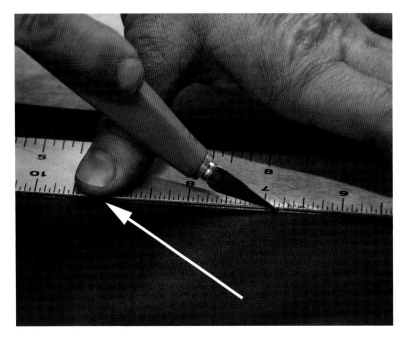

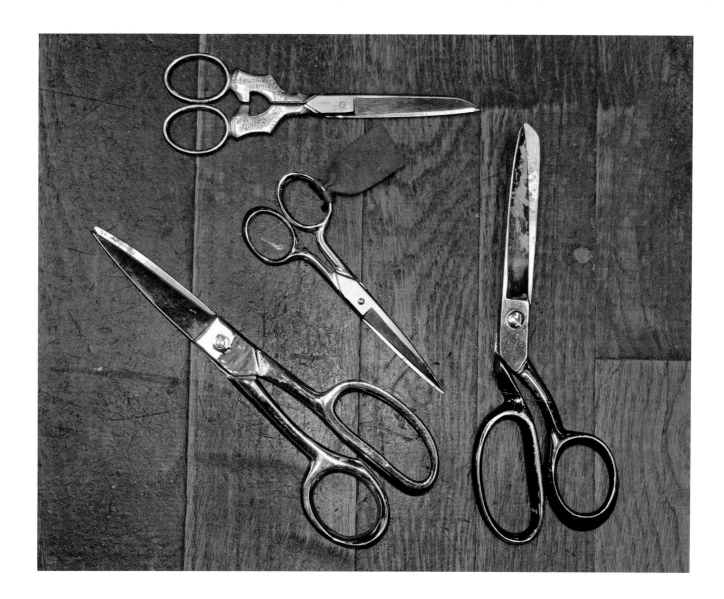

While intricate designs and small pieces must be cut with a sharp, pointed knife for maximum accuracy, scissors work well for large pieces and soft curves. Many boot makers do not consider scissors to be an appropriate leather tool. In fact, when I worked for Jay I was not only forbidden to use scissors at all, I couldn't even have a pair of nippers on my sewing machine to cut threads and had to use a small knife. In my opinion this prejudice against scissors is primarily because of inexperience and/or inability to use them properly.

When cutting out inlay pieces, I mostly use scissors. These are the parts that go behind a precisely cut hole for inlay. These pieces are softly defined, designed to be big enough to fill the hole with a little room to spare so they can be stitched into place. Once they're glued in place and stitched their edges

will no longer be visible, so accuracy isn't quite as critical as the actual design cut into the main portion.

When cutting the actual design into inlay and overlay, accuracy is vitally important. Designs will be transferred onto the leather with powder dots or a silver leather-marking pen. Try to develop the ability to accurately cut outside, exactly on, or precisely inside the pattern lines on the leather—there will be occasions when this level of skill will be necessary.

*When I create a poster board design I punch the holes where the **stitching** will be on the finished product.* Stitching can cause an inlaid design to "grow" because it encircles the design. I want to know exactly how big the completed design will be so I don't get too close to an edge or another design element. On the other hand, stitching is done within an overlaid design. In order to be able to actually stitch directly where the design indicates, I cut slightly inside the pattern marking for an inlaid design and slightly outside the pattern markings for an overlaid design.

CHAPTER TEN

SEWING

ost leather projects are fully lined with another layer of leather. There are considerations to contemplate before deciding if the project will be lined, and an understanding of the purposes and effects of lining leather is required. Lining a project can sandwich and protect leather layers, and it can add weight and stability to a project.

Leather inlay projects should always be lined. This sandwiches the inlay pieces between the main piece and the lining, so the inlay edges that are underneath can't curl or roll. For inlaid pieces, the choices are which weight of lining leather will best enhance the piece, and whether the piece should be stitched before or after lining it. For instance, I line inlaid leather bracelets after stitching so that the back of the bracelet will be clean and smooth, but I line inlaid boot tops before stitching so that the boot tops and linings will be securely fastened together.

Overlay projects don't necessarily have to be lined because there are no edges underneath the piece. Deciding whether or not to line an overlaid piece requires a different thought process. The thickness of the lining leather and the weight or stiffness it would add to the project is always a factor. I would make exactly the same decisions as noted above for bracelets and boot tops, and for the same reasons. However, if I were creating a barstool or motorcycle seat cover, for example, I wouldn't line them. An overlaid upholstery project would be stretched in place over a cushion and never moved or subjected to wear from the bottom side of the piece.

One final note: A heavier lining leather can add a pleasing hint of "puffiness" to a completed design. The lining leather I choose to use for boot tops is 1.5 to 2 mm thick, but it's flexible and relatively soft, not stiff and dense. When I stitch through it, the thread compresses the leather slightly where the stitch line is. The unstitched areas remain uncompressed, and this adds a hint of dimension to the work.

- Added after stitching, lining can hide the stitch lines completely and protect them from wear. Stitching the project first, then lining it, is a good option if a clean, unstitched look and feel is desired.
- Lining a project and then stitching it secures the lining firmly in place, and stitching through the lining leather brings a slight feel of rigidity to the piece.

I use #33 (TEX 30) bonded nylon thread and a size 11 needle for all of my decorative stitching. A common misperception about leather is that it's always thick and substantial, requiring a huge sewing machine, a large needle, and heavy thread. There are applications where this is true but fine inlay and overlay work is not one of them. A strong thread, #33 has enough weight to add visually to a design, but it's not so heavy that it lies like a big rope on top of the leather. Using a smaller thread also allows you to use a smaller needle, which in turn permits finer, tighter stitching. I routinely sew at 16 to 18 stitches per inch, which wouldn't be possible with a large needle.

To do decorative work with leather, the sewing machine presser foot *must* be a roller wheel—it should look like a coin rolling on its side. This "rolling coin" type of presser foot sits to the left of the needle, and because it rolls on its edge, it has the maneuverability to navigate around tight curves. It also allows for a better view of the area being sewn than a regular presser foot, because it sits only off to one side of the needle.

Remember, the purpose of a "presser" foot is to press down the material that's being sewn. If there were nothing to hold the material, the up and down movement of the needle would also cause the material to move up and down.

When sewing along an edge the roller wheel should always be sitting on the material that's being sewn—the stitcher's view should be roller wheel on the left, needle in the middle, and the edge that's being sewn on the right. This way the roller wheel is holding down the material being sewn and the edge is in full view. Reverse this and the view becomes needle, leather edge, and roller wheel from left to right. In this scenario the roller wheel is either running alongside the edge and therefore not holding down the material, or it's sitting directly on the leather edge, obscuring the view and making precision impossible.

When sewing multiple rows of stitching there's no edge to contend with—but the principle of not obscuring the field of vision with the roller wheel still applies. Do not attempt to add multiple rows by sitting the roller wheel on top of the stitching lines already in place. To add multiple rows of stitching, the view from left to right should be roller wheel, needle, and stitch lines that have already been sewn. Reversing this order places the roller wheel directly on top of the stitch lines, which makes accurately adding another row unattainable, since the previous row is not visible.

Incorrect: the roller wheel is hiding previous rows of stitching.

Correct: previously stitched lines of thread are visible.

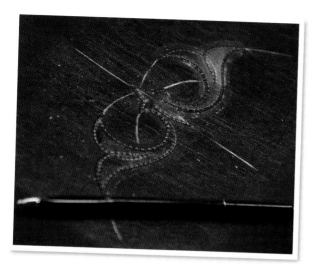

This will be a demonstration of a design with ten rows of decorative stitching. Here I've placed the first two rows and drawn contour lines to direct my stitching around the points.

Two rows of turquoise have been added for a total of four rows stitched.

Two rows of red have been added for a total of six rows stitched.

Two rows of purple have been added for a total of eight rows stitched.

In this final image I've stitched the last two rows in yellow, giving me a total of ten rows, and removed the glue that was holding my pattern markings.

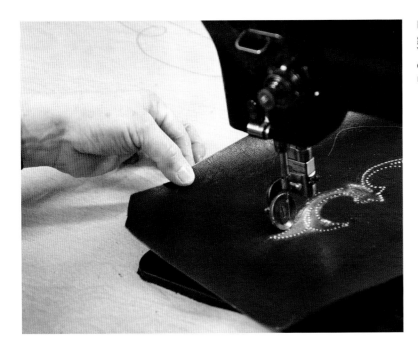

Don't try to stitch a project by gingerly holding onto the edge. You do want to keep your fingers off of the pattern markings as much as possible...

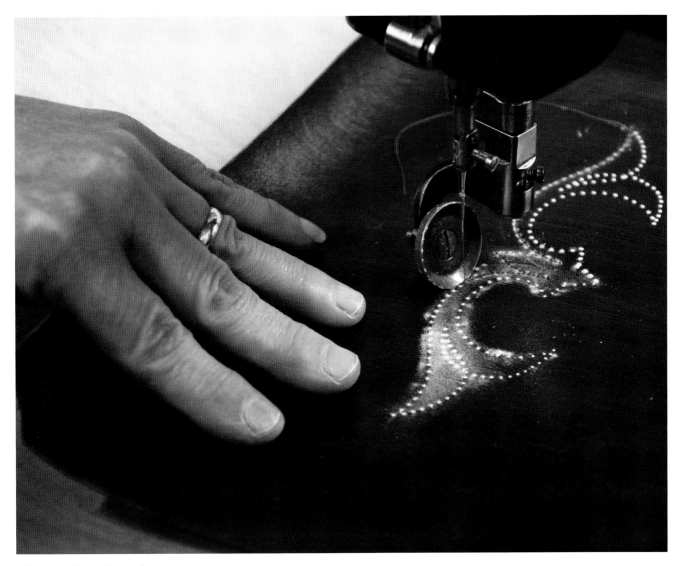

...but use all your fingers for maximum control.

A sewing machine for inlay and overlay work needs to have a knee or foot lift for the presser foot rather than a manual lift. Sewing complex inlay and overlay designs involves many, many changes of direction, each one requiring lifting the presser foot and rotating the work. A knee or foot lift quickly becomes a necessity rather than a luxury. When I found my first job in a boot shop I'd never heard of or used a sewing machine with a knee or foot lift. I quickly grew to love the convenience of it, but it annoyed me that my right foot/leg was working both the feed pedal and the lift while my left foot was doing nothing. I decided to train myself to stitch with my left foot. It took a few weeks to gain the same amount of control as I had with my right foot, but the effort was definitely worth it. Now my right knee or foot is reserved for the lift and my left foot operates the pedal—unless I sew something on a domestic sewing machine. Without a foot or knee lift I automatically go back to sewing with my right foot.

If you choose to attempt this method, be prepared to spend some time practicing. It may take a while to achieve total control as you sew. Also, *be very sure that you don't rest your right foot or knee on the lift.* A knee or foot lift works just like the manual lift—when the presser foot is raised it releases the tension on the thread. If you sew with any amount of pressure on the lift it will affect the tension and the quality of the stitch.

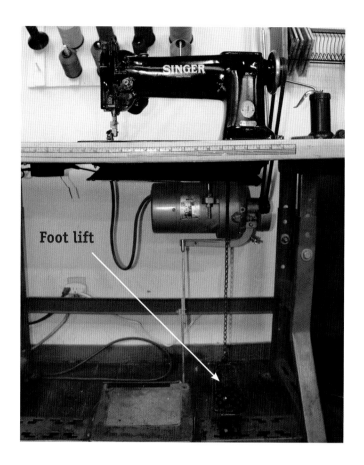

Foot lift

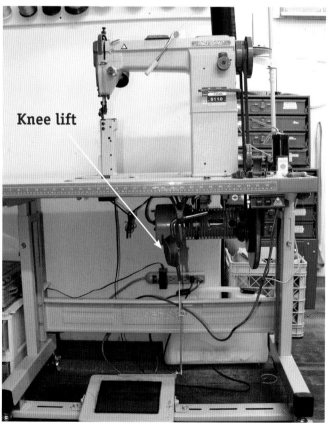

Knee lift

Tension

When my mother began teaching me to sew at age twelve, I vividly remember her instructions regarding tension. She pointed to the wheel and said, "This is the tension wheel—don't ever touch it." That was probably good advice for a beginner, but when you sew different types and weights of leather you *will* need to adjust the tension. The tension adjustment post is on the front of the sewing machine. Various thicknesses of leather will require more or less tension.

The purpose of the tension wheel, and the goal for each stitch, is for the stitch to lock right in the middle of the material being sewn. If the bobbin thread is showing on top of your work, there's too much tension—the top thread is pulling the bobbin thread up to the top of the material. If the top thread is visible underneath the work there's not enough tension; without enough tension the bobbin thread can pull the top thread all the way through the material.

Because the lining leather I use on cowboy boots is a pale cream, I routinely use white bobbin thread. I buy pre-wound white bobbins and don't bother matching bobbin thread to top thread color. This is convenient but it's also dreadfully apparent if the bobbin thread gets pulled to the surface. For this reason I buy Sharpies in every color of the rainbow. A visible spot of bobbin thread will show occasionally and this can be corrected with a quick touch of a Sharpie in the appropriate color.

If the top tension is too loose, the bobbin thread will pull the top thread to the bottom of the material being sewn. Again, because my lining leather is pale if I'm sewing with a dark-colored thread this is horribly visible.

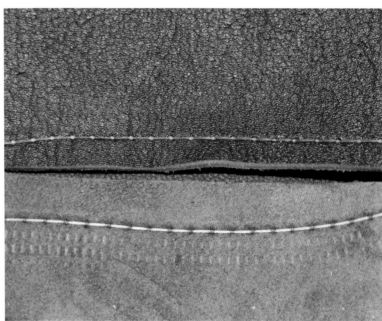

For this illustration I've used orange for the top thread and white for the bobbin. In the top example, the top tension is too tight and it's pulling the white bobbin thread up through the leather. In the bottom example, the top tension is too loose, allowing the bobbin thread to pull it to the underside of the leather.

There's a very precise way of beginning to sew that will allow you to avoid attempting to hold onto the threads as you begin. With the roller wheel raised, lower the needle toward the starting point. Turn the handwheel until the needle pierces the leather *and* the take-up lever is in the lowest position. Grasp the top (not bobbin) thread and from the right, pull firmly until slack at the take-up lever disappears. Bring the top thread around in front of the needle and to the left side. Lower the roller wheel onto the thread and begin sewing. The roller wheel will hold the thread and prevent it from being sucked down into the bobbin as you begin stitching, eliminating the need to hold the threads as you begin sewing.

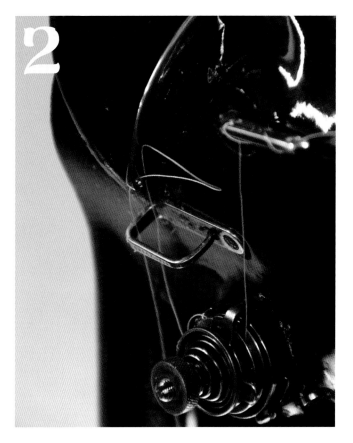

Pivoting

Decorative stitching on leather involves an endless series of points, and a sharp precise point requires a pivot. Sew to the desired point, and then, using the hand-wheel, lower the needle to the lowest point. Continue to turn the hand-wheel *just* until the needle begins to raise. ***Do not raise the needle completely.***

Once the needle begins to move upward, stop, raise the roller wheel, pivot on the needle to face the desired direction, lower the roller wheel, and continue stitching as normal. It's necessary that the needle goes all the way down into the leather and begins to rise again before pivoting, because this sequence completes the stitch. If you attempt to pivot at the point where the needle has entered the leather but not fully descended or begun to raise, the machine will frequently drop this stitch, leaving an ugly stitch-less hole in the leather.

Tying Down the Points

Another technique for decorative leather is referred to as tying down the points. When a piece of leather with a point or a corner is sewn, that corner will tend to roll up unattractively unless it's held down. Taking one stitch over a corner or point is called tying it down.

To tie down a corner or point, sew into a corner to within one stitch from the edge. Finish this final stitch completely—the needle should completely pierce the leather and raise up to the highest point. Make sure the take-up lever is also at the highest point. Using the hand-wheel, lower the needle until it nears the leather but doesn't touch, then raise the roller wheel and move the leather until the needle is positioned to come down directly over the point of the corner. Lower the roller wheel and make a single stitch that ties down that point, and use the handwheel to manually complete this single stitch. Make the stitch completely—the needle should completely pierce the leather and raise up to the highest point. Make sure the take-up lever is also at the highest point. Using the hand-wheel again, lower the needle until it nears the leather but doesn't touch it. Raise the roller wheel again and move the leather until the needle will come down in the hole of the final stitch. Lower the needle into the original hole, turn the work so that it's facing the desired direction, lower the roller wheel, and continue stitching as normal.

Sew right into the corner. RED dot indicates where to stop. Take one stitch directly over the point. Complete this stitch, then raise the lift and move the work over so that the needle will enter at the RED dot again. Turn the work and continue sewing.

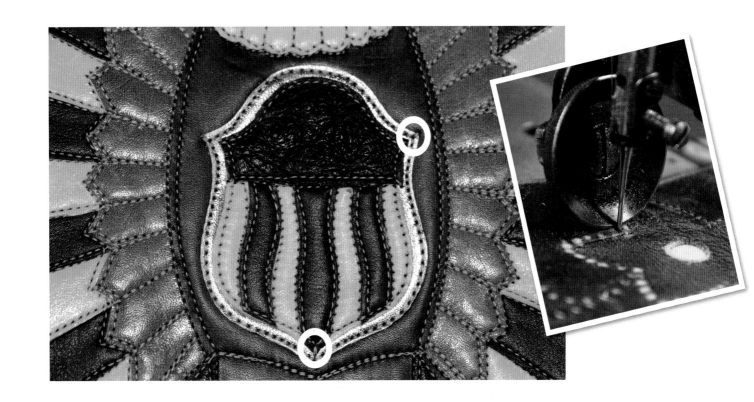

Sewing Curves

Sewing smoothly and accurately around curves requires learning a modified version of the pivoting process. An obvious problem with sewing curves is simply controlling the machine all the way through the curve without swinging wide and losing the desired line. If you manage to achieve this you'll immediately notice the secondary problem: Sewing a concave curve forces the machine to take smaller stitches and sewing a convex curve pulls the machine into making longer stitches.

The only way to avoid either of these stitch-length variations is to make minute adjustments as you navigate a curve. These adjustments are performed by sewing a few stitches, pivoting slightly on the needle, sewing a few more stitches and pivoting again, through the curve until it is completed.

The goal is to create a true curve with no corners and less variation in stitch length. Avoid stitching past the curve and then pivoting to reposition and come back to the curve. This will create a corner. Each pivot and reposition must be very small and must be within the curve radius to be stitched. If these small repositions are done gradually throughout the curve they will create a continuous curve.

Each pivot must be performed by raising the lift and pivoting on the needle. Again, be sure to completely release the pressure on the lift before sewing, to keep tension on the thread. You can either choose to sew with the pressure foot completely down and no pressure on the lift, or you can put pressure on the foot or knee lift and raise the roller wheel—*you cannot do both at the same time*. If you attempt to sew with pressure on the foot or knee lift the machine will draw the top thread down into and under the bobbin case and create dreadful knots. When I'm teaching students to sew, the most common complaint I hear is, "The machine's messing up again!" If I examine a student's stitching and discover that the machine "messes up" directly after a pivot or a tied-down point then I know the cause is always operator error.

This was my very first attempt at decorative stitching. Notice the corners in the curves.

Stopping

After you're through sewing, always stop with the needle fully raised *and the take-up lever in the highest position*. If you stop with the take-up lever down, the next time you use the machine, as you lower the needle into the work, the take-up lever will rise and unthread the needle. This is annoying when you do it to yourself and *extremely* annoying when someone else does it to you, so learn to be a responsible member of society and always stop with the take-up lever in the highest position.

When you've finished sewing and are ready to remove your work from the machine, press the foot or knee lift firmly. This not only raises the roller wheel, it also releases the tension on the thread so as you pull the work out the thread will pull out too.

A note about adhesives and sewing machines: If glue builds up on the sewing machine needle, it will cause the machine to skip stitches. I used solvent-based rubber cement for years and now use water-based Aquilim cements, and I do not have problems with glue building up on my needles. This is not because my sewing machines are special, it's because I'm careful about how I apply glue.

It is very important to remember that glue should be spread out as thinly and as quickly as possible. More glue does not make a better bond, it just adds a sticky layer between leather pieces. Also, when applying glue, spread it out as quickly as possible; don't daub and dither as if you're a painter working on a canvas. Working slowly gives the glue time to begin drying, and pulling a brush through half-dried glue simply spreads sticky clumps of glue. It's also crucial to allow the glue time to dry after bonding and before stitching, as wet glue will adhere to the sewing machine needle.

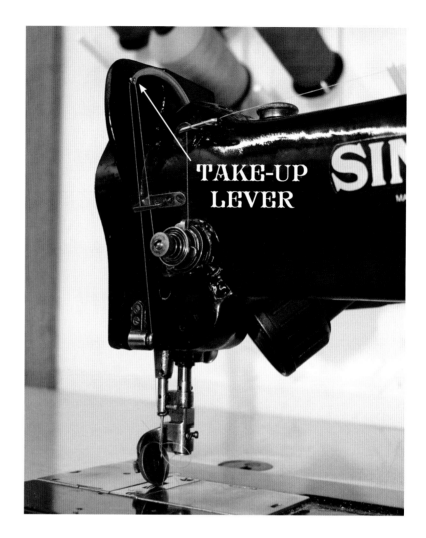

TAKE-UP LEVER

Burning the Thread

Backstitching, or sewing forward, backward, and then forward again, when starting is common when sewing fabric but it would be visible and unattractive for decorative stitching on leather. I was originally taught to pull the top thread through to the back and tie a knot to finish a stitch but I'm not confident of the staying power of knots in nylon thread. That said, one of the advantages to using nylon thread is that it melts.

When stopping or starting a stitch I recommend melting the nylon threads. To do this, start from behind the work and pull the bobbin thread firmly to draw the top thread through the leather and to the back. Insert an awl under the bobbin thread at the final stitch and lift up, then catch the resulting loop of top thread and pull it all the way out to the bobbin side. Cut both threads off short, leaving about 1/16" to 1/8". Hold a cigarette lighter to the thread and burn it until the short ends of thread are molten little blobs, then quickly smash them flat with your finger or the end of the lighter. If the melted nylon is not firmly and completely pressed into the leather while it's hot it will leave a hard knot on the surface of the leather. If it's a piece that will be worn next to skin this knot will be scratchy and irritating.

CHAPTER ELEVEN

BEADING

When sewing with fabric, it's necessary to finish the edges to prevent fraying. Leather edges will not fray, and are typically edged or finished in some way to provide a cleaner look and/or to add another color or dimension. Even if a leather edge is left unfinished it should still be skived; being able to see the thickness and color of the leather under the finish is not attractive. Also, not all leather is the same color all the way through, and an unskived edge allows these color variations to show.

The most common edge finish in cowboy boot making is a beaded edge. Beading is created by wrapping a thin strip of leather around a small cord; the exact same technique in fabric is called piping. Because the beading has a cord inside, it puffs up slightly over the edge of the leather, disguising the unfinished look of the edge. I prefer to make my beading small and delicate, so that it doesn't look like a huge worm crawling along the edge of my project.

I use kangaroo leather for beading because it's thin and doesn't add much bulk. Start by cutting a strip of kangaroo that's ⅝" wide and as long as you need for your project. Although I normally don't measure this, if you don't have the ability to tell at a glance the difference between ½", ⅝", and ¾", then you should use a ruler. Skive both long edges of the kangaroo strip, with a skive as wide as possible for the leather you've chosen.

To make beading, use ¼" double-sided tape. Run a strip of double-sided tape along one edge of the beading strip about ¹⁄₁₆" from the edge. Do not put the double-sided tape directly on the edge of the leather—it should be about ¹⁄₁₆" from the leather edge.

For the center of the beading I use size 346 (TEX 350) nylon thread. I use white because it's a common, readily available color. The color's not important because it's going to be fully enclosed by the leather.

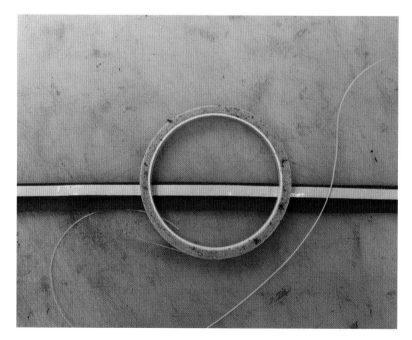

Although double-sided tape is definitely the best choice for making beading, if tape is not available, you can also use glue. Begin by spreading out newspapers or paper to protect your working surface, and then lay the skived beading strip out flat on the paper, flesh side up. Apply a thin coat of rubber cement or Aquilim down the full length and width of the strip or strips and allow to dry. When using Aquilim I find it's helpful to apply the glue and then immediately remove the strips from the paper and allow them to dry spread out somewhere else. Since Aquilim is water based it softens the fibers in the paper. The paper will shred and stick to the leather when the glue dries and the strips are removed.

If you're using the glue method, allow the glue to dry. If you're using tape, remove the paper cover so the sticky tape is exposed.

Begin by placing the beginning of the cord into the center of the leather. Fold about half an inch of leather over the cord, with the cord trapped right in the center of the fold, and press down tightly. This will hold the cord end in place as you work your way down the rest of the leather strip.

As you begin to fold the leather over the cord, press down firmly with the middle finger of your non-dominant hand. As you continue making the beading, press each freshly completed section with this finger, leaving your thumb and forefinger free.

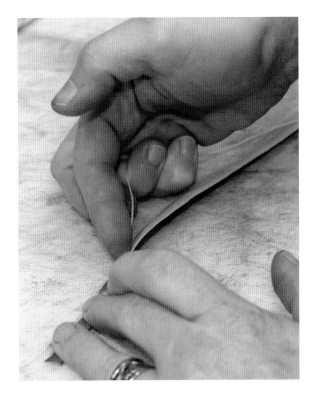

Hold the long piece of cord that will be folded into the beading with the ring and little finger on your dominant hand. The goal here is the ability to keep the cord taut while keeping the thumb and forefingers free on both hands.

When folding the leather over the cord, don't fold it so that the leather edges meet precisely; instead, stagger the leather edges so that one is about ¹⁄₁₆" back from the other. This preserves the skive by keeping the leather edge thin. If you put a skived edge right on top of another skived edge, you've just doubled the thickness of that edge.

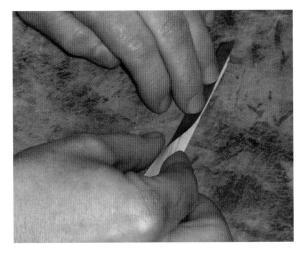

Fold the leather over the cord a little bit at a time. Keep the cord taut as you work, and use the tip of your forefinger to position and hold the cord in the center of the beading strip. As you hold the cord with your forefinger, roll the beading strip over the cord with your dominant thumb, and then press the leather down over the cord with your non-dominant forefinger.

Do not try to carefully lay or glue the cord into the center of the beading strip. It won't stay there and the only result will be frustration. Instead, focus on holding the cord taut in the fold as you make the beading. When the cord is held tightly you can fold the leather over it and make sure it's positioned right in the fold of the leather.

After the leather strip has been folded over the cord, the cord should be snug into the fold of the leather. To encourage and enhance this, run the edge of a hammer head right alongside the entire length of the cord to smooth it up into the fold. The cord should form a well-defined line in the beading, right up in the fold, so that later it will be easy to position it correctly on the leather edge.

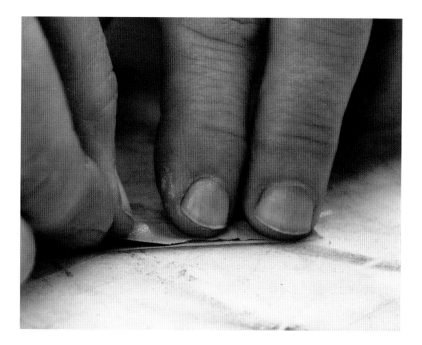

The most important technique for making beading is making very small sections at a time. I work my way down the leather strip by folding about ½" at a time. If you attempt to fold longer sections wrinkles will develop as you fold and it will also be difficult to keep the cord taut and pushed tightly back into the fold of the leather.

Beading should be applied to an edge that's been narrow skived. With care and practice, beading can smoothly bend around corners, and both convex and concave curves. I was taught to attach beading to the leather edge with rubber cement, by applying cement on both the main piece of leather and the beading, but I now use and prefer double-sided tape for this application. Quarter-inch double-sided tape works perfectly for beading made from ⅝" wide strips of leather.

The double-sided tape that I use is clear. It's adhered to a white, waxy paper, but once the paper is peeled away the tape itself is transparent. Some home sewing machines don't like sewing through double-sided tape, but I never have any problems sewing through double-sided tape with my machines. Do not make the mistake of buying double-sided tape that has the look of loosely woven fabric with a yellowish layer of sticky glue. This type of double-sided tape *will* allow glue to build up on the needle and cause problems.

Start by applying the double-sided tape to the beading. The edge of the double-sided tape should lay right up against the bulge formed by the cord. There should not be any distance between the bulge of the cord and tape edge nor should the tape extend over the bulge of the cord. Pull the paper off the double-sided tape when you're ready to put the beading on the leather edge.

When beginning to apply the beading, it's necessary to initially place the beading with the back side of the project facing you. From the back, stick the very beginning of the beading down into the correct position. Once you have the beading end in the correct place turn the

piece over and work from the front.

When positioning the beading, *don't bring the beading up to the leather.* Instead, allow the beading to rest on the work surface and gently lay the leather down into place on the beading. The beading can be bent or curved as necessary, but don't lift it from the table. Just like in making the beading, work in small sections rather than trying to position large portions of the edge precisely on the beading. The leather edge should lay exactly over the double-sided-tape edge, snug up against the bulge of the cord.

The beading cord should be snug under the leather edge. Stitching causes the leather edge to pull inward just a little and allows the beading to squish outward a fraction. The beading should be just a little tighter to the edge than one might initially assume. If the beading is placed too far out from the edge, and then when stitched it moves a fraction farther out, the results will look like a fat worm crawling along the leather edge rather than a neat little line of beading.

If the leather piece that's to be beaded has curves or corners, reliefs will have to be cut into the beading before it's applied to the main piece so that it will conform to the desired shape. To go around a concave curve, cut slits into the beading. This will allow the beading to open up and make the curve. Cut the slit almost to the top edge of the double-sided tape. A very sharp curve will require more slits cut closer together but a gentler curve won't need as much. Too many are better than too few—I usually cut slits about ³⁄₁₆" to ¼" apart.

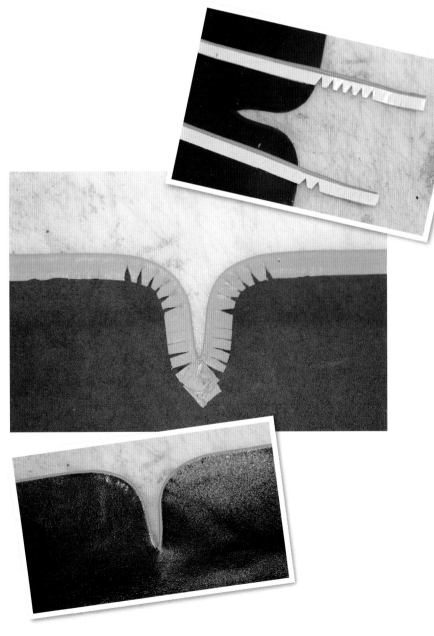

When you put beading around a convex curve it can bunch up and create wrinkles. To prevent this, cut triangular reliefs out of the beading, again cutting these reliefs almost up to the edge of the double-sided tape, and spacing them similar to the slits for concave curves. I wish that I could recommend pinking shears for this application, but I've never been pleased with their performance. The teeth are narrower than the double-sided portion of the beading, so either the triangles don't extend all the way up to the tape edge or part of the thin, skived edge is trimmed away, and I don't like either of those options. If I could find pinking shears with really wide jagged teeth I would happily recommend them for this application.

Going around a sharp corner requires

cutting one large, precisely positioned triangle out of the beading edge. Lay the leather edge onto the beading and determine exactly where the corner needs to be cut. Mark the tape with a dot where the corner needs to be, then cut a triangle. The point of this triangle needs to extend to the edge of the double-sided tape and stop right under the bulge of the cord. If it's not precisely positioned and cut all the way up to the cord you won't get a nice corner.

After cutting the triangle, fold the beading so that it creates a sharp corner. The triangle shape that's been removed allows the beading to turn and make a corner without bunching and wrinkling.

After the beading has been applied to the leather edge, and before stitching, tap it firmly with a smooth flat hammer to compress and smooth it to the leather. Pay special attention to corners or areas where two pieces of beading join. Any bulges in the beading will affect the accuracy of your stitching. The first priority in eliminating these bumps and bulges should be good skiving, but it's surprising what a few firm taps with a hammer can do to smooth and flatten leather.

The backing, or lining, piece of leather

should always be cut larger than the work, leaving a margin to be trimmed after stitching. There's a special leather tool for this called a common edger—I prefer either size 1 or 0. This tool accurately trims away the excess leather without risk of cutting the beading. A more readily available tool that will also accomplish the same task is a fabric seam ripper.

The blade of the common edger is in the shape of a V and the blade of a seam ripper is in the shape of a U. When trimming with either of them, one side of the blade should run right beside the stitch line. Do not attempt to trim with the stitch line in the center of the V or U: that will result in cutting too close to the stitching and slicing the thread.

Be sure to keep a faint downward pressure on the tool so that the work does not lift up off the table. It's impossible to trim a smooth edge if the leather being trimmed is moving about in mid-air. As you trim, hold the excess that's being trimmed away and keep it taut as you slice away the excess leather. This can feel like an awkward maneuver at first because you have to reach over the hand that's holding the edger in order to grasp the leather being trimmed away.

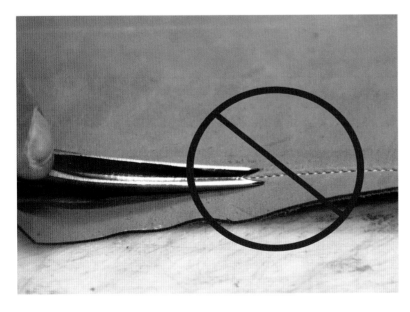

CHAPTER TWELVE

ADDITIONAL TECHNIQUES

Folding

A folded edge is quite common in shoemaking. I rarely ever use the technique in boot making but it is a necessary skill to have. Instead of beading, an additional allowance is added to a leather edge. This allowance is then folded over to finish the edge. Rather than adding an additional strip of beading, the edge itself is folded.

When the leather edge is folded over, the challenge is making sure to fold over both the correct amount *and* the same amount all along the edge. For kangaroo leather, a ¼" folding allowance is common. If you've planned for an additional ¼" that will be folded over, you want to make sure that it's precisely ¼" and not ⅛" in places and ⅜" in others.

To make a folded edge with ¼" turned under, measure in from the edge ¼" on the back side of the leather. This is the fold line. Create another line that's ½" from the edge. We'll call this the secondary line. When the ¼" folding allowance is folded into place, the outermost edge of it will touch the secondary line. The leather edge will need to be skived, but wait until you've marked these lines before skiving. Once the lines are marked onto the back of the leather, skive the edge with a ¼" wide skive. Using the fold line as a guide, create a skive that starts exactly at the fold line.

Put ¼" double-sided tape on the leather edge or apply rubber cement up to the secondary line. Fold the leather over, making sure the outermost leather edge precisely lines up with the secondary line.

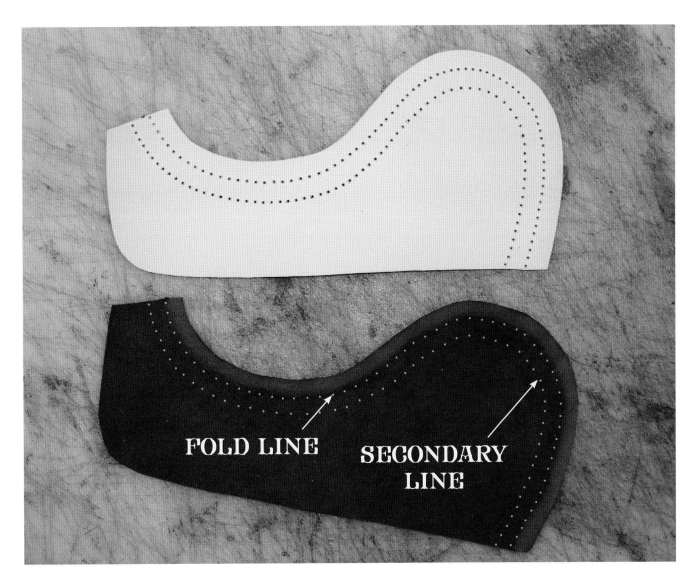

FOLD LINE   SECONDARY LINE

Just like with beading, it will be necessary to cut small slits into the leather when going around a concave curve. Don't cut the slits all the way to the fold line; if you do it will create "corners" in the smooth line of the curve. Instead, cut the slits about two-thirds of the distance to the fold line. The slits will allow the leather to open and create a smooth line around the curve.

When making convex curves with folded edges, I don't cut triangle reliefs into the leather as I would for beading. If the leather has been skived well, any wrinkles created by folding should smooth out and not be visible from the front.

I find that it's helpful to fold a leather edge with an awl rather than your fingers, especially for convex curves. Fold the leather down to complete the folded edge in any straight areas, but leave the curve unfolded. Starting at the very center of the curved area and using the awl, fold the middle of the curve down to the line. Push the awl flat against the leather so that only an awl's width

is stuck together. Now you should have a curve with a small bit stuck down right in the center of the curve.

You now have two unfolded curves, one on each side of the area that was pressed down with the awl. Move to the center of one of these areas, fold the edge to the line, and press it firmly with the awl again. Repeat on the other side. Work back and forth repeatedly, always starting in the center of a section and pressing only an awl's width each time, until the entire curve is stuck down. You should be leaving small "pipes," or tunnels, of leather that grow increasingly smaller as you work your way around the curve with the awl. Once you've worked your way completely around the curve and the pipes are as small as possible use a hammer to gently tap them flat. If you've worked back and forth in small increments you should end up with a smooth curve, sometimes being able to eliminate any creases at all. Corners are only created when you attempt to fold too much leather at once as you go around the curve.

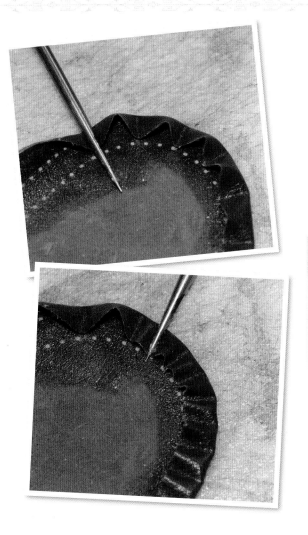

Gimping

Gimping creates a decorative edge on the leather by cutting a repeating shape into the leather edge. Stationery stores frequently have paper-cutting scissors, similar to pinking shears, that cut various types of decorative edges in paper. I've always assumed that these specialty scissors aren't durable enough for leather so I haven't tried them, but perhaps they would work.

A gimped edge is often left unskived. In my shop I have several options for creating a gimped edge. I have a little hand-cranked, bench-mounted gimping edger that I bought on eBay, a gimping attachment that fits into my post machine, and gimping punches. Pinking shears also work well for gimping edges.

This is a gimping tool that I bought on eBay.

It cuts a wavy leather edge.

Gimping punches are inexpensive but working your way down an edge with a single punch is time consuming.

I prefer to create a gimped edge with the sewing machine attachment. This interchangeable piece fits into the needle bar. Adjust the stitch length for the gimping tool and position the gimping attachment so that it almost touches the throat plate of the machine. Position a thin but firm piece of leather under the leather edge to be gimped. The gimping tool should be positioned so that it pierces the leather edge but doesn't pierce the backing leather. If the gimping tool hits the throat plate it will break or bend the edge and dull it.

Adjust the stitch length on the sewing machine so that it will create the gimped look you desire. Lay the leather you want to gimp on top of the firm backing leather and run the machine slowly. The gimping tool will cut through the top piece of leather, creating a shaped edge. The bottom piece of leather is there to support the top leather and also to prevent the gimping tool from hitting the feed dogs or roller wheel and breaking, dulling, or bending.

A gimping attachment fits into a sewing machine in the place of a needle.

Cording

Laying a piece of cord behind leather is another interesting way to add dimension. To create a raised design, apply a thin coat of rubber cement to the back of the leather, mark the design over the cemented area, and press cord along the design. It's helpful to apply rubber cement to the cord also but can be a messy procedure! After the cord is stuck to the leather all along the design line, cut a thin piece of leather that's big enough to cover the entire corded design, skive it all the way around, and cement it into place covering the cord.

Turn the piece over and **working from the front**, press the two layers of leather together, also pressing the leather firmly up to each side of the cord. This will define the corded design. Use a tool that's rounded and smooth so it won't damage the leather finish as you run it firmly along the cord. The best tool that I've found for this operation is the type of pencil that has a metal top in place of an eraser.

It's tempting to press everything down from the back once the lining leather has been added but this would be a mistake. The cord creates a lovely raised appearance only on the side that's pressed flat around it. If you work from the back you'll have a nice raised cord on the back of the leather and a flat, barely visible design on the front.

In order to define the cord and keep it in place permanently, it must be stitched on each side of the cord. It works best to keep corded designs rather simple; there must be room for the roller wheel to maneuver on each side of the cord. Make sure that the roller wheel is on the flat area of the leather and the needle is right up next to the cord. The roller wheel should *not* be sitting on the cord.

It's possible to add dimension to the work by adding a layer of something "puffy" under the work. This layer should be trimmed to be slightly smaller than the design element it enhances. You want something soft enough to sew through but with enough body to add volume. I find make-up sponges to be the perfect texture, and they can easily be trimmed with scissors to the desired shape.

I glue the sponge or stuffing material to the back of the overlay piece. It's necessary to cut the stuffing material about ¼" smaller than the overlay piece. There **must** be a margin of leather around the stuffing to adhere to the main body of the piece. If the stuffing is the same size as the overlay piece the edges won't stay down as you're attempting to sew. If the stuffing is the same size as the overlay piece there might also be an issue with bits of stuffing sticking out, which wouldn't be at all attractive.

Buck Stitching

Buck stitching, or lacing, is commonly done with a very narrow strip of leather, usually ⅛" to ³⁄₃₂" wide. It's generally used along an edge, but this is not the only option. Holes are punched into the leather and the lacing goes over and under, mimicking stitching.

While the technique for all buck stitching is the same, the look can be varied by the size, shape, and position of the holes. The hole can be a slit that's the same width as the leather lacing. These slits can be parallel or angled toward and away from each other. My personal favorite technique is to punch holes and lace through those. If the holes are smaller in diameter than the width of the lacing, the lacing compresses as it comes through the hole and then spreads out to full thickness, creating an interesting effect.

One of my favorite design techniques is punching a series of small holes along an edge. While hole punches are often used for small design details such as bird eyes and flower centers, punching a series of holes along a leather edge is a traditional detail that's commonly used in cowboy boot making. The holes are called perforations, so adding the holes would be referred to as perforating the leather.

When using a hole punch, position a heavy piece of leather or rubber under the leather being punched. Don't use a plastic cutting board for a punching surface—it's too hard and will break or bend the fragile punch blade. A softer surface such as leather or rubber will yield a cleaner cut without damaging the punch blade. Also, don't hit a punch with a hammer. It probably won't hurt the top of the punch but it will mar the hammer face. If you later use that hammer to tap leather layers together, the marred face can cut or mark the leather. Always use a rawhide or plastic mallet for hitting a hole punch.

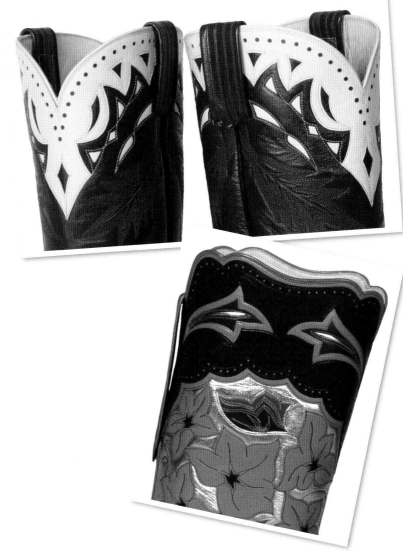

Roses can be created by twisting or wadding up the leather to create folds. A thin, soft leather works best for this technique and I recommend using regular solvent-based rubber cement in this instance.

To start, create your pattern and draw the shape of the rose you want to make. This is very important because the rose will be defined only by the shape of the hole you cut for it. For this type of pattern, instead of using the sewing machine to define the rose shape, cut the shape out of the poster board pattern. Cut a circle of leather larger than you need and apply rubber cement to the back side of the piece. Allow the rubber cement to dry completely, then flip it over and apply rubber cement to the front side as well. Allow this application to dry too.

Once the cement is dry, grasp the center of the leather firmly between your thumb and forefinger and pinch the leather up and around in the twisting motion. The goal is to create multiple lines of wrinkles, so separate any large flat wrinkles that try to develop. Work the leather into multiple wrinkles and then press them down firmly so they'll stick together and stay in place.

Lay the poster board pattern with the rose-shaped hole over the wrinkled leather. Position and reposition it until you're satisfied with the wrinkled "rose" leather that appears in the hole. Using a silver pen, trace the edges of the rose-shaped hole onto the wrinkled leather. Remove the poster board pattern. Draw another line with the silver pen that's about ¼" larger than the defined rose already drawn onto the leather. Cut off the excess leather at this line.

Working from the front, skive off the wrinkles from the first silver line out to the edge. Be sure not to skive inside the first line of silver. That line defines the part of the rose that will be on display, so if you skive inside it you'll be removing part of the visible rose. Now turn the rose over and finish skiving from the back. The challenge in making twisted roses is going from multiple wrinkles of leather to absolutely smooth edges that blend invisibly as inlay. Skiving from both the front and the back makes this easier.

Once you've skived the front and back, you can glue the rose into the project. Before

proceeding, skive again on the excess wrinkles from the back. Feel with your fingers around the rose edges and check for thick bumpy areas that need to be thinned before stitching.

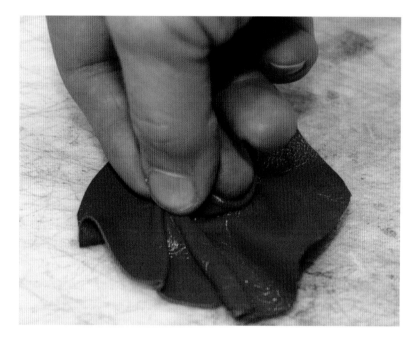

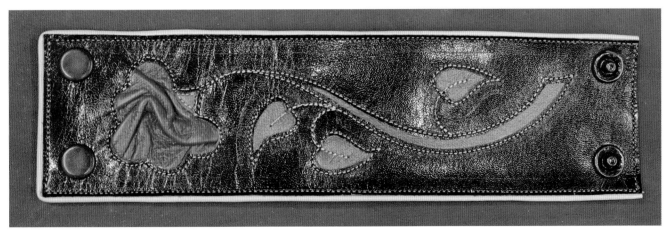

CHAPTER THIRTEEN

SEWING MACHINES

ost cowboy boot makers use either a Singer 31-15 or a 110W machine to stitch their boot tops. Both models are old machines and they're still readily available, often with the original table and motor. I still do all of my inlay, overlay, and multiple-row stitch patterns on my Singer 110W that I bought when I left Jay Griffith's shop. The original motors on these machines are clutch motors and require dedicated practice to develop control.

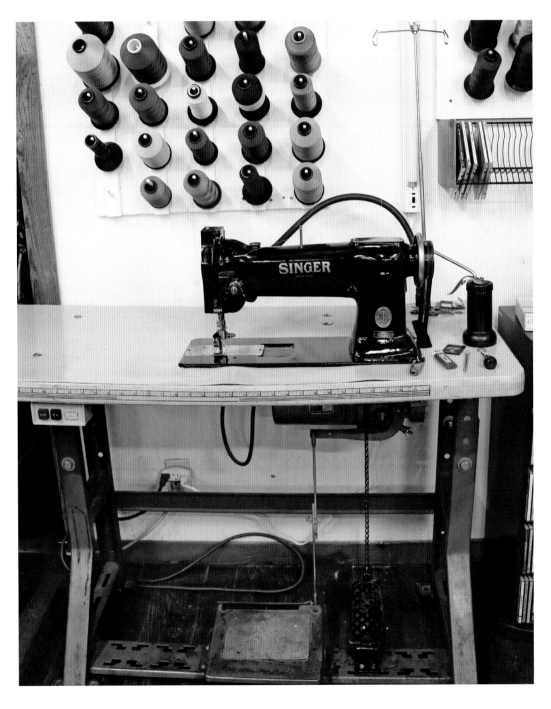

Because these machines are old they frequently have worn parts, and it can be difficult to find original replacement parts. Some sewing machine dealers sell original parts from old machines; these are occasionally just as worn as the part you're replacing. Some dealers sell new parts for the old machines, but often these parts are cheaply made and frequently don't work or perform as well as they should. On the bright side, these are well-made old machines with good metal parts; it takes a lot of use to wear them out.

There are two major differences between the Singer 31-15 and the Singer 110W. The 31-15 has an infinite stitch length adjuster on the front; it will adjust from zero up to around 5 stitches per inch. The 110W has three gears and therefore only three stitch length options. These gears can be switched out to attain the desired stitch lengths. I have gears in my machine for 12, 15, and 18 stitches per inch.

The second distinction between the two machines is the way the material is fed through as it's stitched. The 31-15 uses traditional feed dogs to move the material, whereas the 110W has a roller feed wheel. The roller wheel slowly revolves to feed the material, resulting in a smooth and continuous movement, as opposed to feed dogs, which move the material with an up-forward-down, up-forward-down motion. The movement of feed dogs is not as smooth as the roller wheel, and it's the reason I prefer a Singer 110W with a roller feed wheel.

Machine with infinite stitch length adjustment lever.

Machine with three gears defining stitch length options.

Roller feed wheel

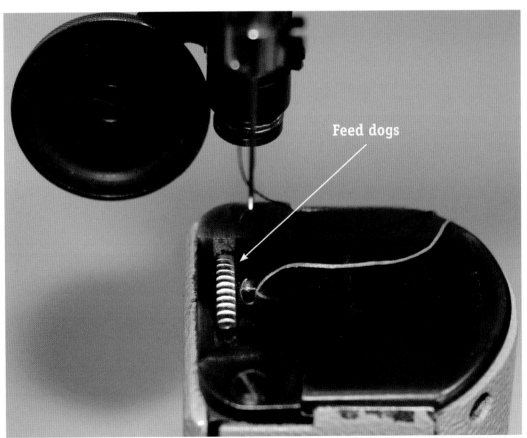

Feed dogs

Many of my students are opting to purchase a new machine, which I encourage—when things go wrong (and they will) it can be difficult for a novice to know if the problem is operator error or a worn machine. Also, while the less expensive new machines are made in China (and are nowhere near the quality of the old Singers), at least you can still buy parts for them. I own two new Chinese-made machines and I'm quite happy with each of them.

Newer machines will have a servo motor. This type of motor is quieter and easier to control than the old clutch motor. They also frequently have a function that allows you to reduce the maximum sewing speed, and therefore reduce the chances of accidentally pushing too hard on the pedal and quickly sewing through something you didn't intend to sew: for example, your finger.

If you decide to purchase a new machine, don't allow yourself to be talked into one with features you don't need and that will not make your sewing experience better. Students in my shop will use a basic post machine for all decorative stitching, and this is the type of machine I encourage them to buy. It's a very simple machine, it's easy to adjust the timing, and the motor can be adjusted from slow to fast. The only "extra" it has is a reverse feature, and I rarely use that. It has feed dogs rather than a roller wheel, but so far I haven't found a new sewing machine I like that's available with a roller feed system.

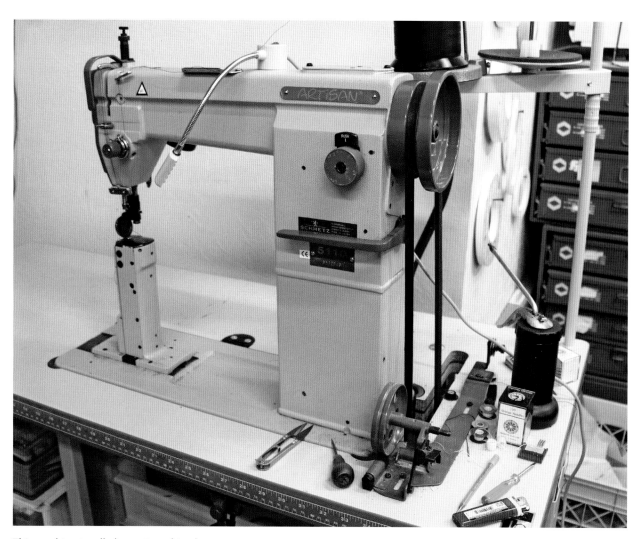

This machine is called a post machine because the bobbin mechanism is raised up in a post. It works exactly like a flatbed machine but the post allows the user to sew in small or awkward areas.

A roller wheel presser foot is absolutely essential for doing any sort of decorative stitching on leather. It looks like a coin rolling on its side and can range from about three-quarter to one inch in diameter. Usually the edge will be grooved to help it grip the leather.

In order to advance the leather through the machine, it has to be held tightly between the feed dogs/feed wheel and the roller presser foot. This pressure can sometimes leave an impression on the leather, but these grooves usually disappear through time and/or wear. Occasionally the presser foot is adjusted to press too tightly against the feed dogs. There should be a large screw on the top of the machine that can be turned to reduce presser foot pressure, or turned the other way to increase pressure. I've also seen some roller wheels with no grooves—I assume in an attempt to reduce the potential for marking the leather. The ability to feed the work doesn't appear to be affected by eliminating the grooves, but these wheels still leave an impression on the leather, so I haven't found them to be an improvement.

Don't be influenced by the wonders of a gear-driven roller foot if you only plan to use your machine for decorative work. With this feature the presser roller wheel has its own separate driving gear so it feeds independently of the feed dogs. I made the mistake of thinking this design would help solve the problem of stitch length variations when navigating curves. It helps marginally on curves where the stitch length tends to shorten. However, on convex curves, when the stitch length tries to lengthen, it makes the problem worse because it enthusiastically pulls the work around the curve, increasing stitches even more than normal.

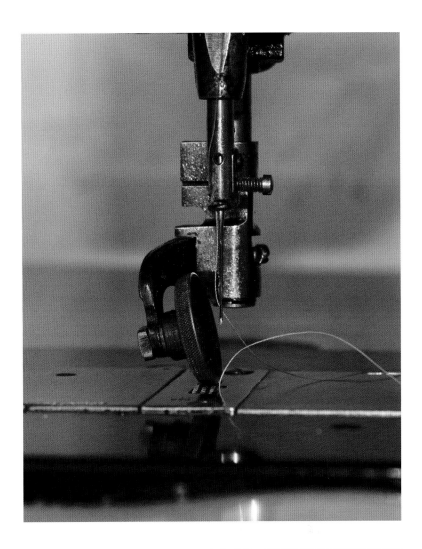

The tension adjustment is located on the front of the sewing machine. As the machine is threaded, the thread goes through two discs that are positioned like this:)(. A screw in front of these discs can be tightened to bring the discs closer together and pinch the thread tighter, putting more tension on the thread, or loosened, for less tension on the thread. The purpose of the tension wheel, and the goal for each stitch, is for the stitch to lock right in the middle of the material being sewn.

The entire tension system needs to be taken apart and cleaned every now and then. Fuzz from the thread eventually builds up between the tension discs and begins to hold them apart no matter how tightly the tension is adjusted. If your studio is neat and clean, you won't need to do it very often, but if the thread spools or cones are dusty the fuzz will accumulate between the tension wheels frequently and require regular cleaning.

Remove the tension components one at a time, laying them out in order so you can remember and see how to put them back. Clean the inside of the tension wheels and replace everything back onto the tension post in the reverse order that they came off. I usually just wipe the debris off of the tension discs with my finger, but if they're terribly dirty, a cotton swab dipped in acetone will clean off all of the gunk.

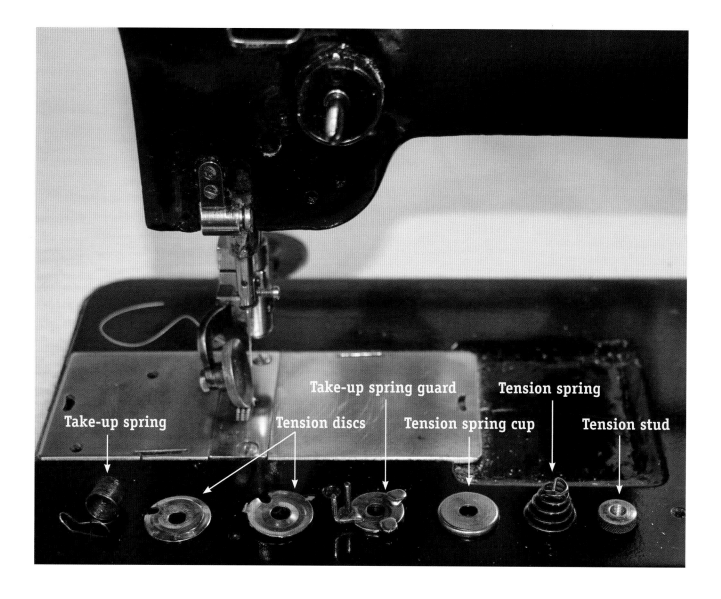

Take-up spring Tension discs Take-up spring guard Tension spring cup Tension spring Tension stud

Turn the screw on the tension post clockwise to tighten the tension and counter clockwise to loosen the tension.

Replacing the take-up spring and the discs can be a bit tricky. The base of the spring goes in first and the discs are inserted in the middle of the take-up spring opening.

When the tension is adjusted properly the loop of the stitch should be in the center of the material being sewn. When the top tension is too tight it will pull the bobbin thread up through the material with every stitch. If the bobbin thread is showing on top of your work there's too much tension—the top thread is pulling the bobbin thread up to the top of the material. When the top thread is visible underneath the work there's not enough tension. Without enough tension the bobbin thread can pull the top thread all the way through the material.

There is a tension screw on the bobbin case and occasionally it has to be adjusted, but it is very rare. As a rule, all tension adjustments can be made using the top tension alone. If you determine that the bobbin thread does need to be adjusted, do so in the smallest of increments. This tiny little screw is only ¹⁄₁₆" long. An enthusiastic adjustment will either tighten it down all the way or loosen it right out of the bobbin case, and this is not a screw that you want suddenly dropping to the floor. I can testify to tediously long sessions of crawling around on the floor, hoping to spot the tiny bobbin case tension screw, and worried I'd never find it.

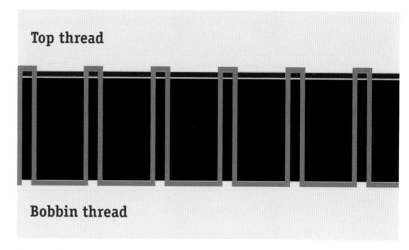

Too much top tension.

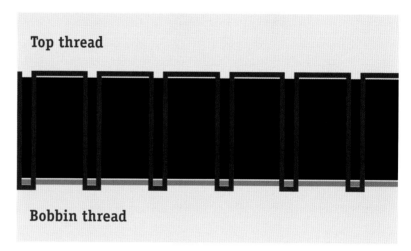

Not enough top tension.

It is my belief that anyone who owns and uses a leather sewing machine should be able to time it. It can be hard to find a sewing machine manual for the old Singers and the "English" manuals for the Chinese-made machines are hilariously unhelpful. Therefore I'm including information about how a sewing machine should be timed and how to adjust the timing if it's not sewing properly.

The obvious sign that your machine is not timed properly is skipped stitches. An immediate cause of this can be distorting the needle (usually as you try to navigate a curve) and therefore breaking it by hitting the needle plate. If the needle hits the needle plate hard enough it can knock the machine out of time.

To check the timing on your machine remove the throat plate, lower the needle to its lowest point, and then raise it $\frac{3}{32}$". At this point the tip of the shuttle hook should be in the center of the needle and $\frac{1}{16}$" above the eye. Many machines have two lines scored onto the needle bar. The top line should just barely be visible when the needle is at its lowest point, and the second line is $\frac{3}{32}$" below it. If your machine has these markings then raise the needle so that this second line is just visible, before the needle bar goes all the way up into the machine. It's at this point that the tip of the shuttle hook should be in the center of the needle and $\frac{1}{16}$" above the eye.

These machines all work on the same basic principle. There's a long bar underneath the machine that connects the feed wheel mechanism with the bobbin/shuttle area. This bar has a gear at the end, directly under the bobbin area. There's another bar that extends down from the shuttle. It also has a gear on the end. These two gears touch. When you push the pedal it turns the first long bar; as it turns it rotates the gear on the bar extending up the shuttle, allowing it to turn.

In most of the older flatbed machines the gears are inside a metal case. There's a hole in the front of the case. As you turn the handwheel the shaft rotates and bring the screws into view so you can loosen and tighten them.

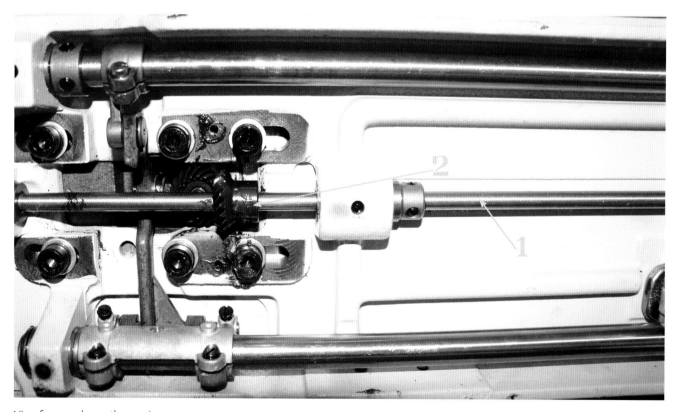

View from underneath a sewing machine. Label 1 shows the long bar that extends the length of the machine. Label 2 marks the gear with two screws attaching it to the bar. Loosening these two screws allows it to slide on the bar, away from the gear that drives the bobbin.

To change the timing of a machine, loosen the gear on the long bar. Once it's loose you can reposition the shuttle as needed so that it lines up correctly with the needle. Make sure the needle is in the proper position—all the way down and then ³⁄₃₂" back up. If your needle bar does not have markings, or if they're in the wrong place, you'll need to improvise. I keep a fine-point Sharpie in my machine drawer along with a tiny strip of poster board that I've trimmed to ³⁄₃₂" wide. When I've lowered the needle bar to its lowest point, I position the poster board strip right up against the bottom collar holding the needle bar and make a mark on the needle bar at the bottom of the poster board strip. This enables me to raise the needle bar to the mark I've made with the confidence that I'm raising it exactly the required ³⁄₃₂".

Rotate the shuttle until the point of the hook is exactly in the center of the needle.

Once you feel that you have both the needle bar and the point of the shuttle hook aligned properly with each other, re-tighten the screws on the gear on the long bar. When you're tightening the screw holding the bottom gear to the long bar underneath it's helpful to keep one hand on the shuttle system, holding it in place as you tighten the screw. This eliminates the possibility of it rotating slightly when you tighten the screw. I will admit that it's difficult to both hold the shuttle in the correct place and tighten the screw on the gear.

At this point the only way to confirm you've timed the machine correctly is to sew something. Don't despair if you don't get it timed correctly the first time. When I first began timing my own machines, I'd often have to time and re-time about 10 to 12 tries before it would finally be right. It's frustrating, but it's a part of the process of learning your machine until you intimately know the machine's every whim and mood.

There are two factors that in rare instances can affect timing—sewing speed and material thickness. The precise guidelines given above are for timing a machine normally. If the shuttle hook is positioned so that it's slightly ahead of the needle when it's lowered and then raised $3/32$" the machine would be timed "fast." If the shuttle hook is slightly behind the needle, or not yet quite at the $3/32$" position, then the machine would be timed "slow." If the machine is timed a little fast and you're sewing very slowly with constant pauses and stops, you're going to experience skipped stitches.

Material thickness can affect timing but it's not a common problem. If the material is extremely, unusually thick it can require a machine to be timed slow, with the needle bar positioned so that the point of the shuttle hook is slightly more than $1/16$" above the eye. In all of my years of sewing I've only had to retime my machine once to accommodate working with heavy leather. *I've never had to time my machine fast for any reason.*

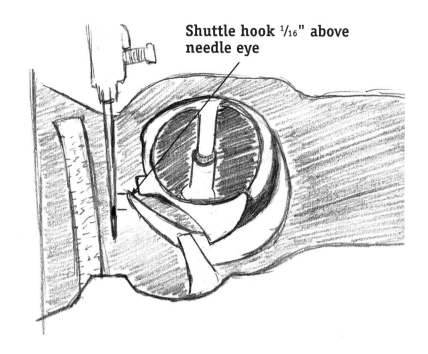

Shuttle hook $1/16$" above needle eye

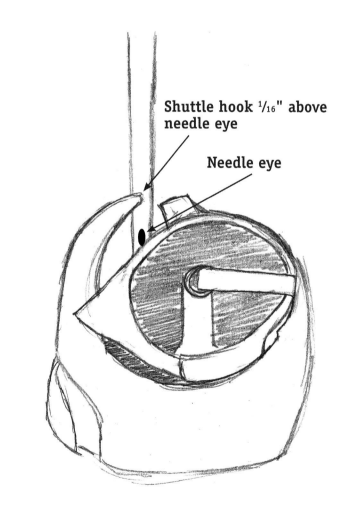

Shuttle hook $1/16$" above needle eye

Needle eye

Thread and Bobbins

I use bonded nylon thread for all of my leather projects. Nylon thread is strong and resists fraying. For decorative work such as inlay, overlay, and multiple rows of stitching, I use #33 thread, also known as TEX 30 or T-30. This is a small-diameter thread and it can be difficult to find in a wide range of colors. Most cowboy boot makers that I know have converted to using a size 46 (TEX 45 or T-45) nylon thread but I still prefer the delicacy of the smaller size.

I also use #33 bonded nylon bobbins. One of my favorite things about learning to work with leather was discovering pre-wound bobbins. I wound many, many bobbins during my years sewing clothing and I've been very happy to give that up. As with top thread, it's easier to find pre-wound bobbins in #46 than in #33.

I always put a few drops of lightweight sewing machine oil in the shuttle area *and* on the bobbin thread every time I change the bobbin. Oiling the thread itself sounds unusual, but it helps the thread feed smoothly through the shuttle and won't hurt the leather. If you have an issue with the bobbin thread pulling up onto the surface of the leather and making a small knot whenever you pivot on the needle, and adjusting the tension doesn't seem to help the problem, try oiling the bobbin thread with a drop or two of sewing machine oil.

I use White brand sewing machine oil; it's lightweight and colorless. After the machine is freshly oiled, the oil will often show as a dark spot on the leather for the first few stitches. This dark spot fades within a few minutes; in all my years of experience I've never had an oil spot become a permanent spot.

SIZE CHART FOR BONDED NYLON THREAD

LETTER SIZE	TKT SIZE	TEX SIZE	RECOMMENDED NEEDLE SIZE
B	33	30	75/11
C	46	45	80/12
D	69	70	90/14

Needles

There are advantages to using the smallest needle possible for the work and the thread size. The stitching on leather will look rough if the thread is too big—like a huge rope lying across the surface—and a larger thread will require a bigger needle.

If the needle is too big it will make large holes in the leather. A large needle dictates a longer stitch length; if the stitch length is too small, the needle will actually begin to cut the leather. Also, larger needle holes act like a black hole when you're sewing multiple rows. The previous needle holes will grab your needle and draw it into the previous row, forcing you to leave extra-wide spacing between rows.

Use the smallest-size needle that will work with the thread size you've chosen. I would recommend a size 11 needle for #33 thread, a size 12 needle for #46 thread, and a size 14 needle for #69 thread. If you're in doubt about whether or not a needle is big enough to accommodate a thread size, cut a length of thread and thread it through a loose needle. Hold the thread with your thumb and forefinger at either end and see if the needle will slide freely from one end to the other. If the needle slides freely, it's large enough to work with the thread.

Using the proper needle system is essential to the sewing machine working properly. Each machine requires a specific needle system and there are many, many different needle systems. A new machine will include information about which needle system is required. The needle system number will be in this format: #×#, as in 16×2 or 135×8. When in doubt, enter both your machine make and model and the words "needle system" into an internet search engine and you should be able to identify which needle system a particular machine requires.

There are three primary bits of information about each type of needle: the needle system, the size of the needle, and the type of point. I use and recommend a size 11 needle, which is also called a #75. A size 12 needle is a #80, a size 14 is a #90, a size 16 is a #100, and so on.

Home sewing machine needles are flat on one side at the top of the needle and therefore only fit into the machine one way. Industrial machine needles are round at the

top and can be inserted backwards or sideways into the machine. If you look closely at the needle you'll see that one side has a groove that runs the length of the needle and the other side has a flat spot above and below the eye. The flat spot should face the bobbin and the side with the groove should be on the opposite side of the bobbin area, facing the roller wheel. Inserting the needle improperly will result in knots, skipped stitches, the inability to create a stitch, and a strong desire to throw the machine out a window.

If you begin to have problems with the thread fraying as you sew or you can hear the needle hitting the leather as it sews, you probably have a dull needle or a needle with a burr on it. When the very tip of the needle is bent, that's a burr. You can feel it by running your finger over the needle tip. It should be smooth and sharp, and not have a catch at the very tip. Sometimes you can take a very fine piece of sandpaper and gently sharpen the tip of the needle again. If the problem continues, throw the needle away and replace it with a new, sharp needle.

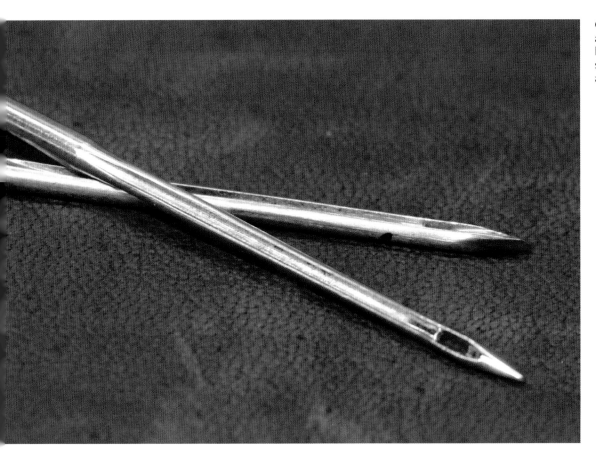

One side of the needle has a groove that runs the length of the needle. This side should face the left, away from the bobbin.

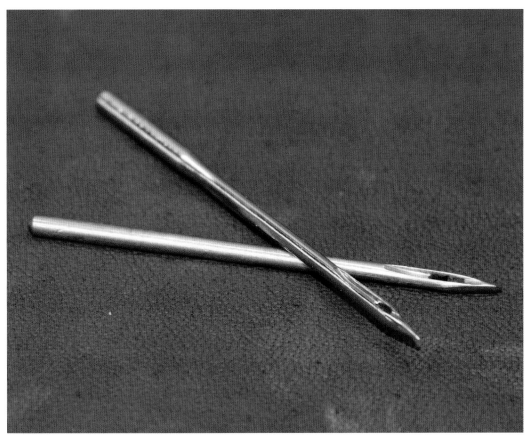

The opposite side of the needle has a flat area around the eye. This flat spot should face the bobbin side of the machine.

CHAPTER FOURTEEN

PROJECT PATTERNS

Bracelet Templates

X SMALL SMALL MEDIUM LARGE

● : Snap placement
   Use this guide to position snaps
   at both ends of the bracelet.

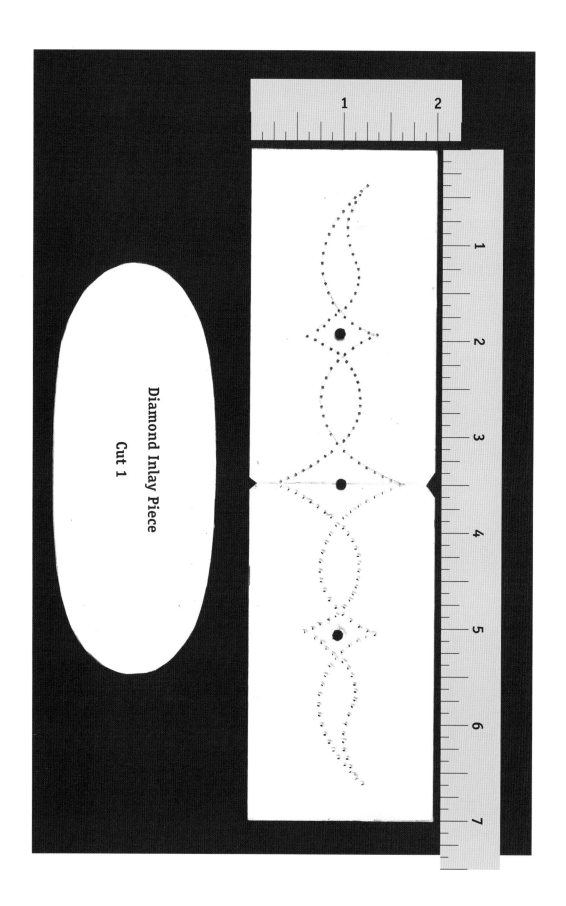

Diamond Inlay Piece

Cut 1

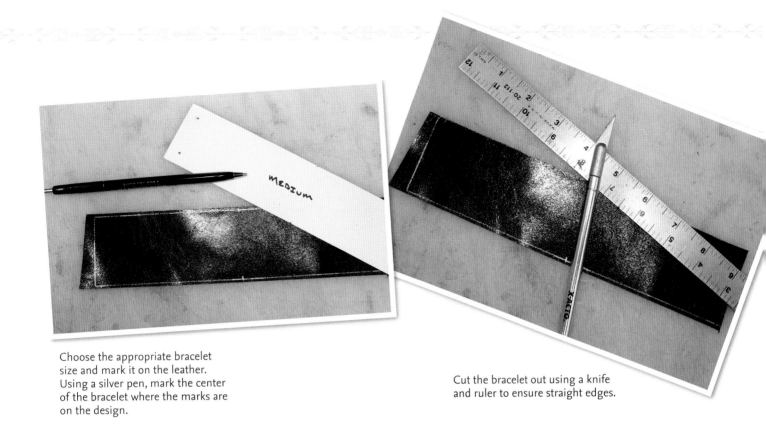

Choose the appropriate bracelet size and mark it on the leather. Using a silver pen, mark the center of the bracelet where the marks are on the design.

Cut the bracelet out using a knife and ruler to ensure straight edges.

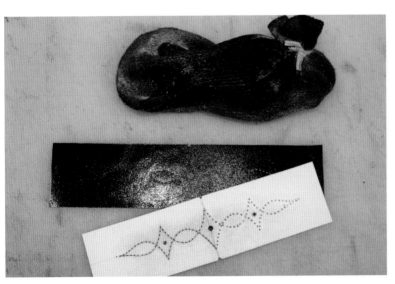

Line up the design with the center marks on the bracelet so that the design will be centered no matter what size bracelet you're making. Rub the powder bag over the pattern to transfer it to the bracelet.

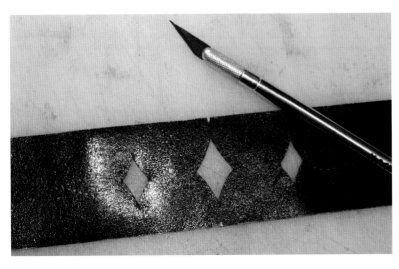

Following the white dots as a guide, cut out ONLY the diamond shapes with an X-Acto knife.

Narrow skive all edges of the bracelet. Also narrow skive all edges of the diamonds. A ¾" skiving knife works well for this.

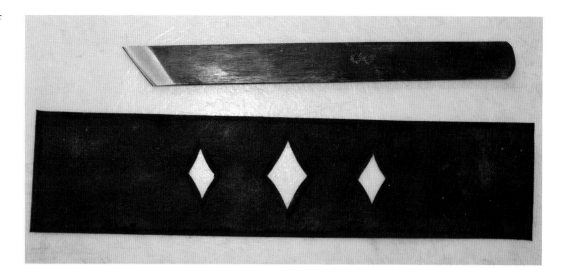

Using the template provided, trace around the inlay piece for the diamonds. Carefully cut out the inlay piece using either scissors or an X-Acto knife.

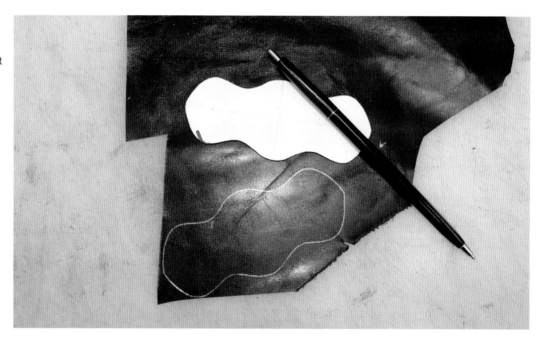

Wide skive all around the diamond inlay piece.

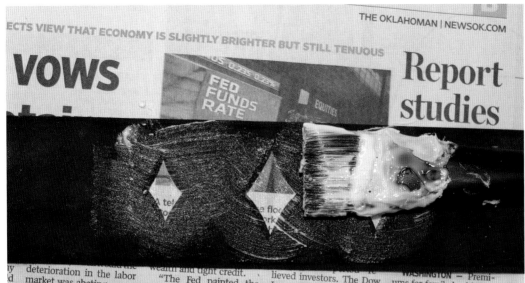

Apply a thin coat of Aquilim SG to the back of the bracelet in the area of the diamond shapes.

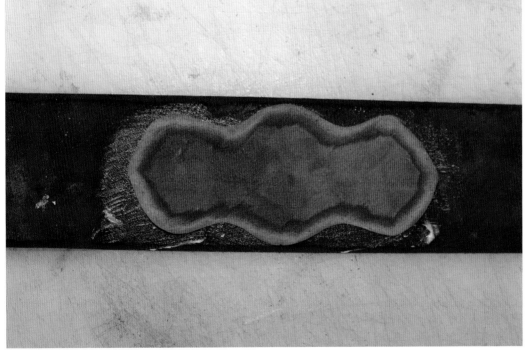

Lay the diamond inlay piece centered behind the cut-out diamonds.

For the dots in the center of the diamonds, cut a strip of leather 4" long and ½" wide. Wide skive this strip on each side.

At an angle, skive off three diamond shapes. Don't worry that one skive is on the back side of the piece and one is on the front side. This is a quick and easy technique to fill in any small bits of inlay.

Position the pattern on the bracelet and rub the powder bag over it to mark where the diamond center holes should be punched.

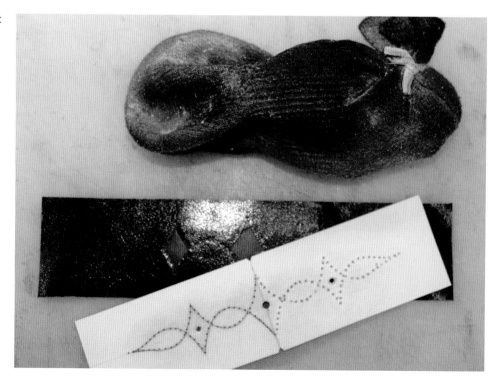

Using a small hole punch and a rawhide or plastic mallet, punch the center holes out of the diamonds. Always use a thick piece of leather or rubber as a backing when punching holes.

Apply Aquilim SG in the area behind the punched holes.

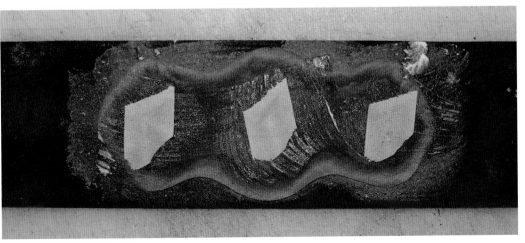

Place the skived pieces behind each center hole.

At this point the bracelet should look like this.

In preparation for stitching, rub the powder bag over the back of the bracelet to neutralize the stickiness of the glue. This prevents the leather from sticking to the machine and dragging as it's being sewn.

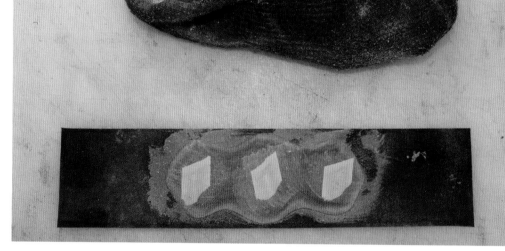

Now position the pattern on the bracelet front and powder it again to mark the stitching lines onto the bracelet.

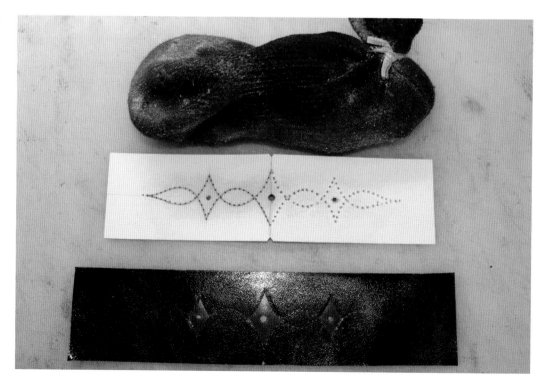

Follow the powder dots to stitch the bracelet design. Always make sure the roller wheel is positioned like the example on the left. In this example the inlay edge is visible, serving as a guide for stitching. In the example on the right the roller wheel is on the wrong side of the inlay, covering the edge.

Mark the bracelet lining pattern onto the lining leather with silver pen and cut it out with scissors or an X-Acto knife.

Apply Aquilim GL to the back of the bracelet and immediately lay it onto the bracelet lining. Lightly tap the bracelet and lining together, wait a few minutes for the glue to dry, then stitch around all four edges.

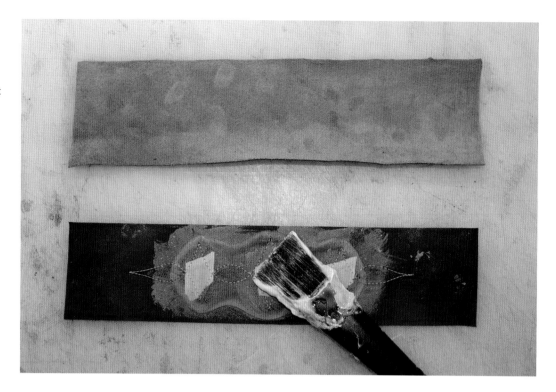

After stitching, use a metal ruler to trim the excess lining leather. Be very careful not to cut too close to your stitch line.

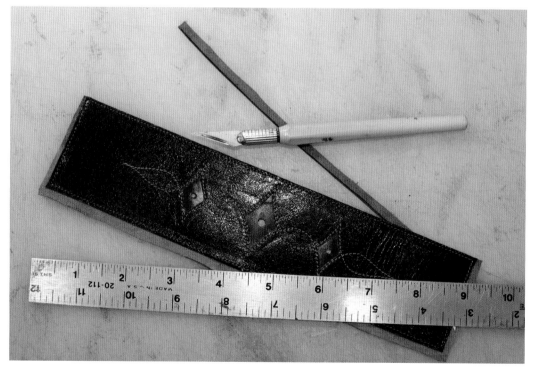

Using the bracelet pattern, mark where the snaps should be positioned. Use an awl to make the marks on the top side of the bracelet at one end and on the lining side of the bracelet at the other end. The awl marks show where to position and place the snaps.

Clean any excess glue from the bracelet with a rubber eraser. Place the snaps at both ends of the finished bracelet and don't forget to sign and date it on the back!

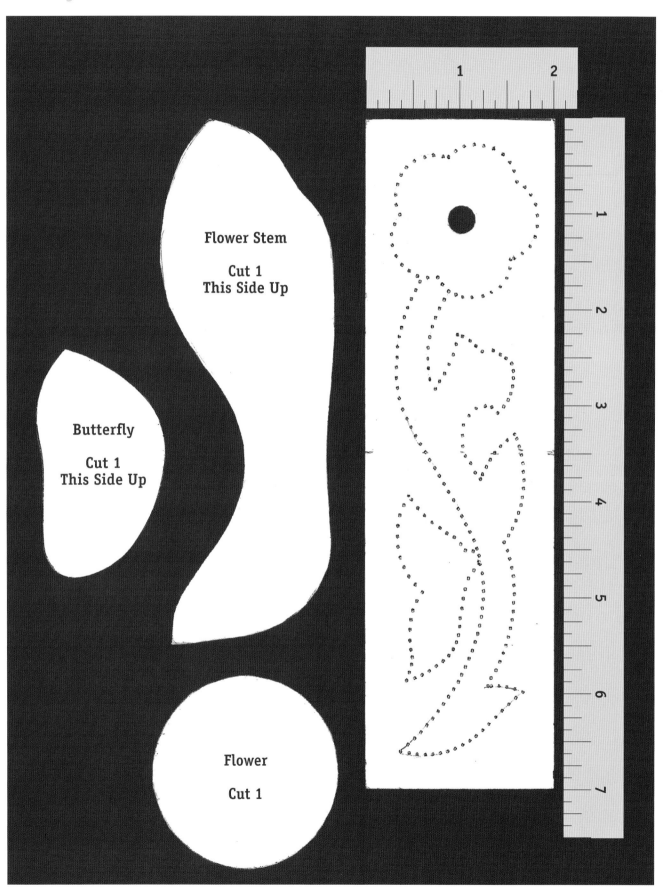

Flower Stem

Cut 1
This Side Up

Butterfly

Cut 1
This Side Up

Flower

Cut 1

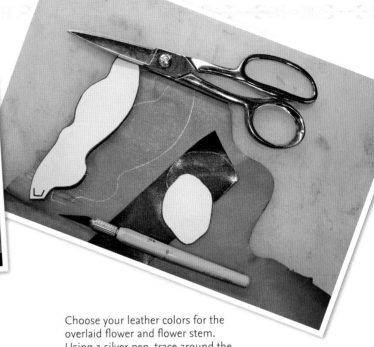

Choose the appropriate bracelet size and mark it on the leather. Cut it out using a knife and ruler to ensure straight edges. Using a silver pen, mark the center of the bracelet at each edge where the marks are on the design.

Choose your leather colors for the overlaid flower and flower stem. Using a silver pen, trace around the flower and flower stem patterns. Cut the pieces out with scissors or an X-Acto knife.

Mark the flower stem and flower on the correct leather pieces. Use a powder bag—a sock filled with baby powder—to rub across the design. Powder will fall through the holes leaving a line of little white dots as a guide for cutting.

Carefully cut out the shapes with a sharp X-Acto knife.

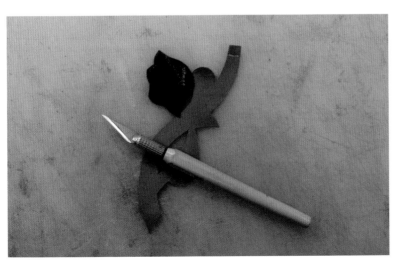

Narrow skive all edges of the flower stem, flower, and bracelet.

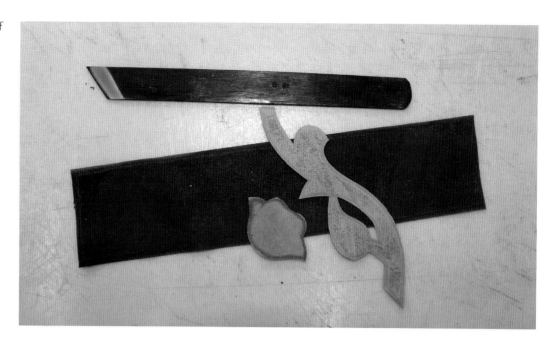

Line up the design with the center marks on the bracelet so that the design will be centered no matter what size bracelet you're making. Rub the powder bag over the pattern to transfer it to the bracelet.

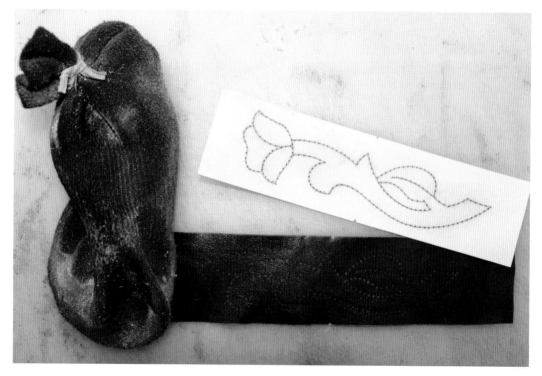

Apply Aquilim SG to the backs of both the flower stem and the flower. Carefully position first the flower stem on the bracelet, and then the flower. The flower stem should extend slightly under the flower.

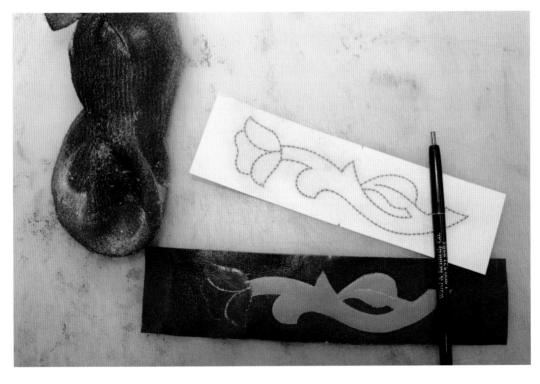

Center the design on the bracelet and rub the baby powder bag over it again to transfer the accent stitching lines in the flower and leaf. Trace these lines with a silver pen if necessary so they'll be visible as a guide for stitching.

The goal in stitching is to start in one place, stitch the entire design, and finish back in the starting spot. While that's not always possible, it is with this design.

When you come to the leaf and flower accent lines, stitch them, then turn around and stitch over the same line until you're back in place to continue stitching the overlay edges.

The completed stitched design should look like this.

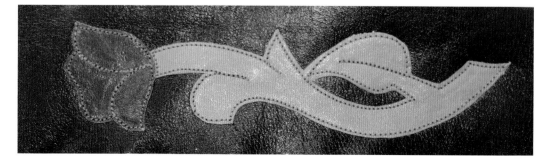

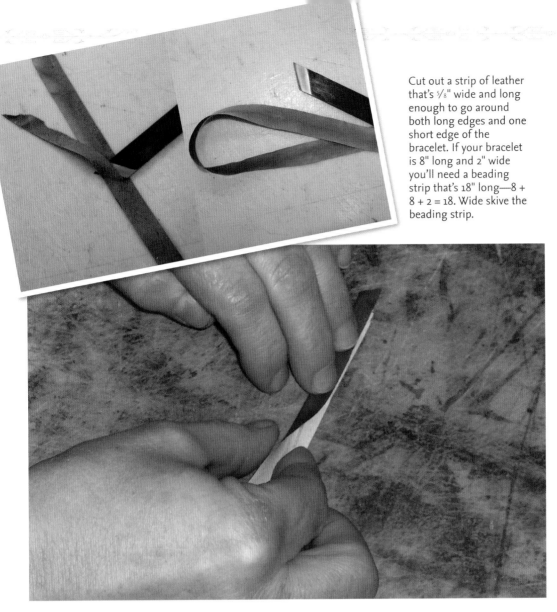

Cut out a strip of leather that's ⅝" wide and long enough to go around both long edges and one short edge of the bracelet. If your bracelet is 8" long and 2" wide you'll need a beading strip that's 18" long—8 + 8 + 2 = 18. Wide skive the beading strip.

Apply double-sided tape to one long edge of the beading, ⅛" from the edge. Pull the paper off the tape and fold the leather in half over a cord to create beading. When folding, line up the top edge with the edge of the double-sided tape, *not* the leather edge. Tip: Hold the cord taut and work in small sections— ½" at a time.

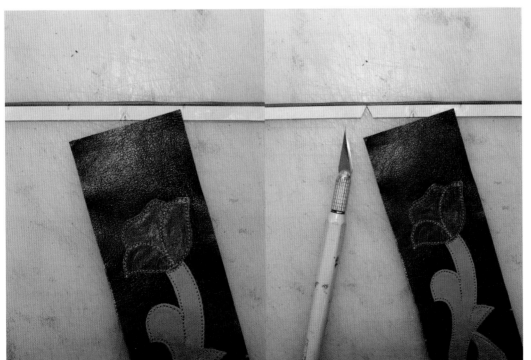

Apply another strip of double-sided tape to the completed beading strip. Position it right next to the rounded cord. Fold the beading strip in half to find the middle. Position the bracelet in the center and carefully mark *exactly* each corner. Cut a triangle out at each mark that extends right up to the enclosed cord.

Fold the beading strip at the cut-out triangles to create a corner. If the cut-out triangles were positioned correctly the beading should exactly fit around the bracelet. Lay the bracelet on the beading between the corners, then apply the beading down each side. Leave the beading laying flat and bring the bracelet down to the beading a little at a time. Try to only leave the corded edge visible.

Mark the bracelet lining pattern onto the lining leather with silver pen and cut it out with scissors or an X-Acto knife. The bracelet lining pattern is ¼" bigger than the bracelet on all four sides.

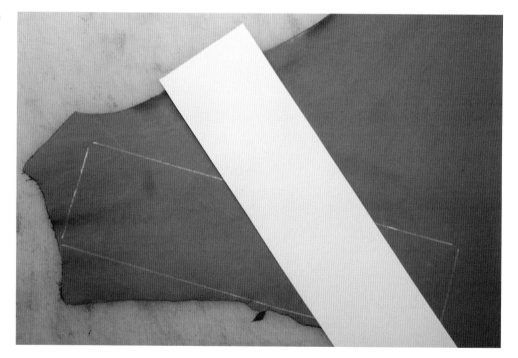

Apply Aquilim GL to the back of the bracelet and immediately lay it onto the bracelet lining. Lightly tap the bracelet and lining together, wait a few minutes for the glue to dry, and stitch around all four edges.

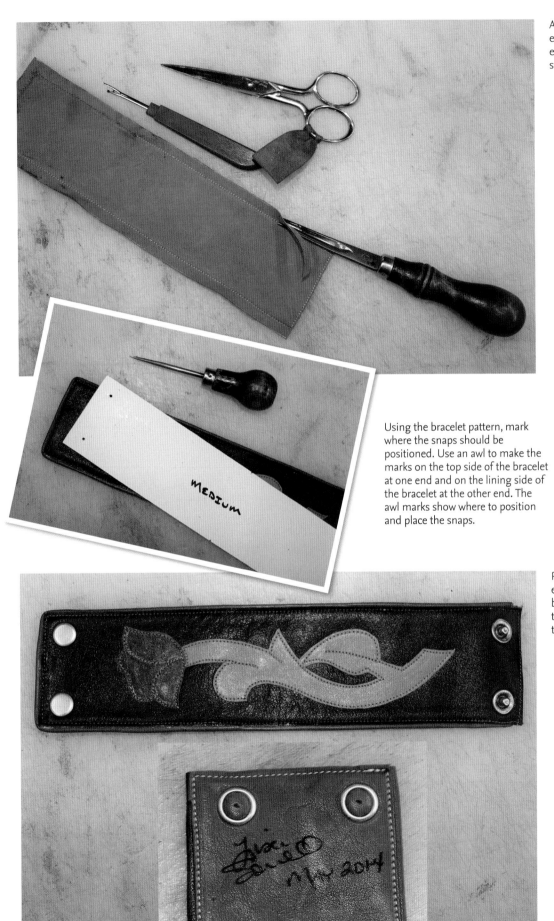

After stitching, trim the excess lining with an edger, seam ripper, or small sharp scissors.

Using the bracelet pattern, mark where the snaps should be positioned. Use an awl to make the marks on the top side of the bracelet at one end and on the lining side of the bracelet at the other end. The awl marks show where to position and place the snaps.

Place the snaps at both ends of the finished bracelet, and don't forget to sign and date it on the back!

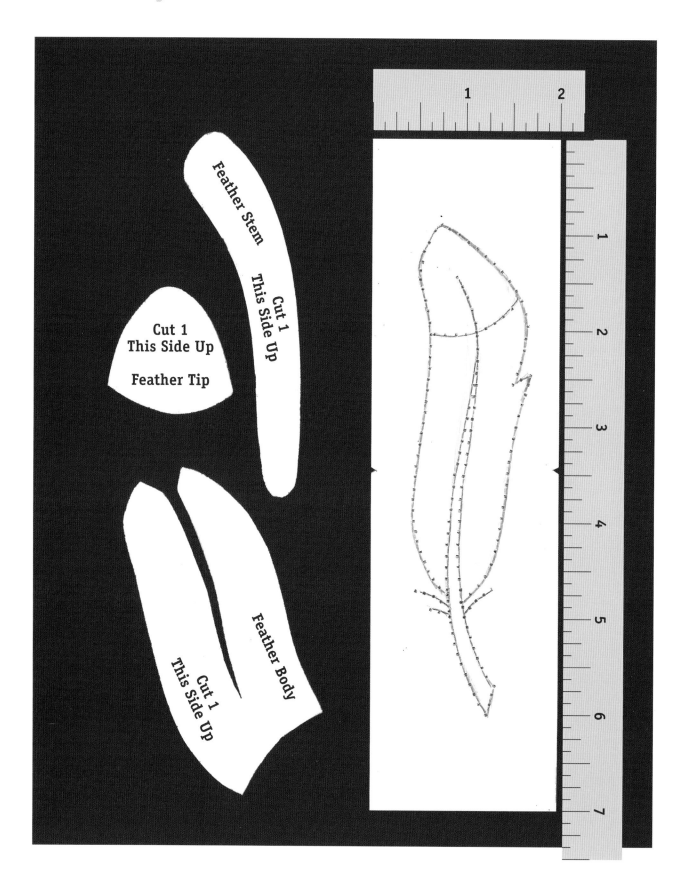

Feather Stem

Cut 1
This Side Up

Cut 1
This Side Up

Feather Tip

Feather Body

Cut 1
This Side Up

1

2

1

2

3

4

5

6

7

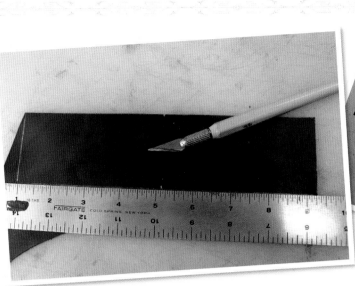

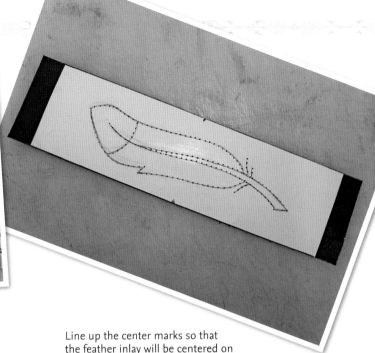

Choose the appropriate bracelet size and mark it on the leather. Cut it out using a knife and ruler to ensure straight edges. Using a silver pen, mark the center of the bracelet at each edge where the marks are on the design.

Line up the center marks so that the feather inlay will be centered on your bracelet no matter what size you've chosen.

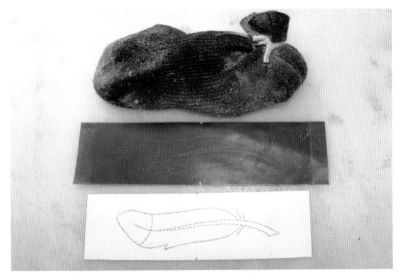

Rub a sock filled with baby powder over the design that's correctly positioned on the leather. The baby powder will fall through the holes, leaving a line of white dots for you to use as guides for cutting out the feather.

Cut out the feather shape using an X-Acto knife.

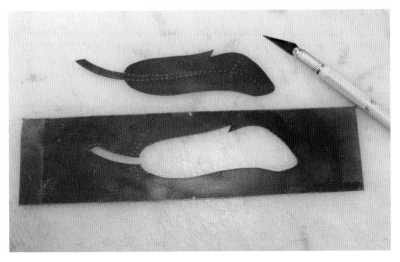

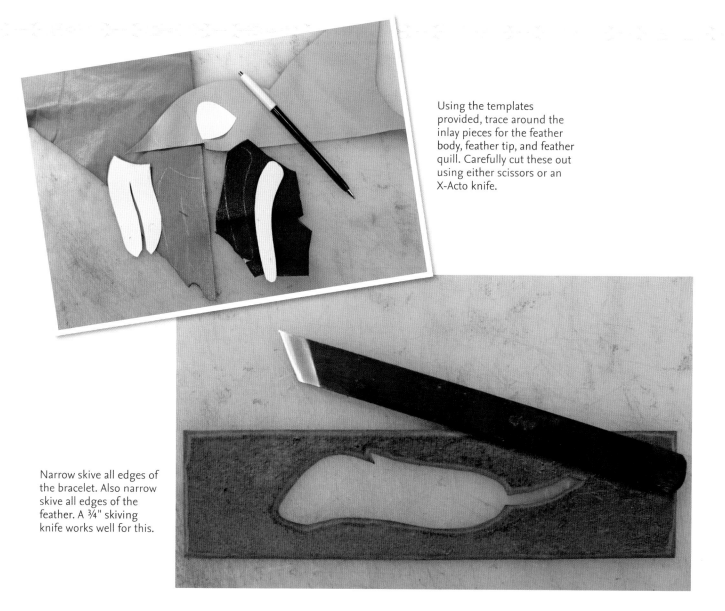

Using the templates provided, trace around the inlay pieces for the feather body, feather tip, and feather quill. Carefully cut these out using either scissors or an X-Acto knife.

Narrow skive all edges of the bracelet. Also narrow skive all edges of the feather. A ¾" skiving knife works well for this.

Skive all edges of the feather inlay pieces. Pay attention to which edges need to be narrow skived and which need to be wide skived. These distinctions are noted on the templates.

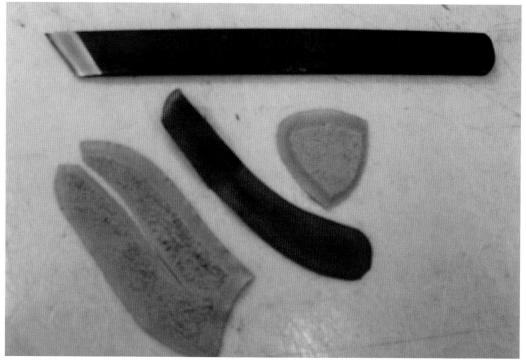

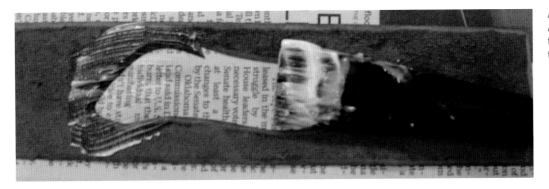

Apply a thin coat of Aquilim SG to the back of the bracelet in the area of the feather.

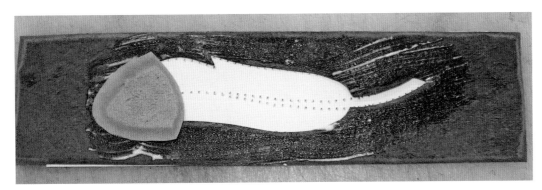

Lay the feather bracelet, glued side up, on top of the bracelet design. This way you can make sure the leather doesn't distort as you're working. It will also provide a guide for positioning the feather tip, which is the first inlay piece to be added.

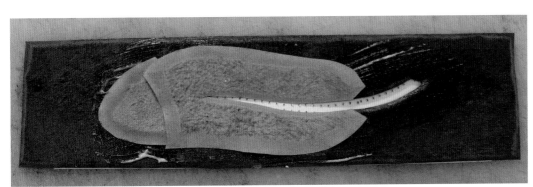

Next add the feather body inlay piece. Again, the bracelet design provides a guide for properly positioning the inlay piece.

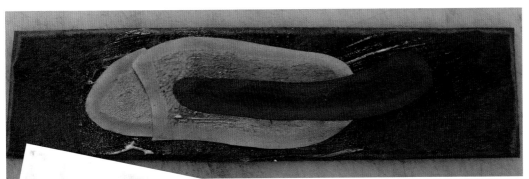

Before adding the feather quill inlay piece, remove the bracelet from the pattern piece and apply a thin coat of Aquilim SG in the area where the feather quill inlay piece will be positioned, lay it back in place on the pattern, and continue.

Gently tap all of the inlay pieces so they'll adhere properly together and to the bracelet. Rub the baby powder sock over the back of the bracelet to neutralize any glue not covered by inlay. The next step is stitching, and fresh glue will drag on the machine plate and cause problems.

Needle = ●

Roller wheel = ▮

Start here, at this corner

First, stitch around the entire outside of the feather. When you get back to the corner where you started, take one stitch off as if you were tying down the point.

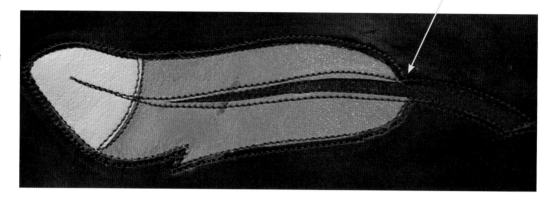

Follow the orange arrows as you stitch up and around the feather stem.

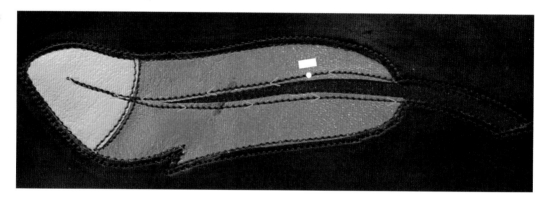

After stitching the entire feather stem, turn and follow the blue arrows to stitch inside the feather. When you are around the tip of the feather you'll take a detour and follow the red arrows across and back to stitch the feather tip.

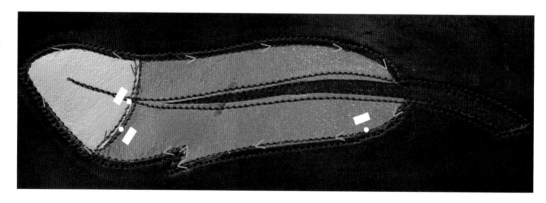

After stitching the inside of the feather, you'll arrive back at the corner where you started. Take one stitch down onto the feather stem and follow the pink areas to stitch inside the feather stem. This will again lead you right back to the corner where you started, completing the design.

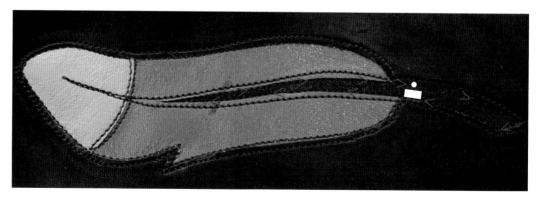

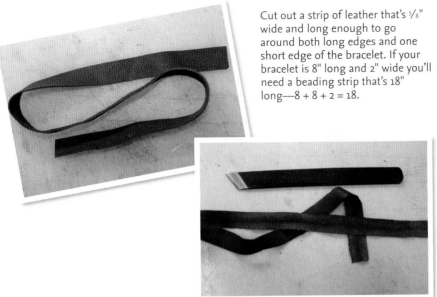

Cut out a strip of leather that's ⅝" wide and long enough to go around both long edges and one short edge of the bracelet. If your bracelet is 8" long and 2" wide you'll need a beading strip that's 18" long—8 + 8 + 2 = 18.

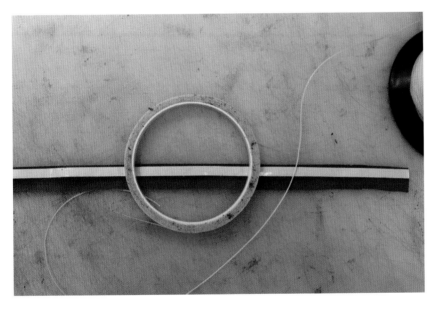

Skive the beading strip with a wide skive.

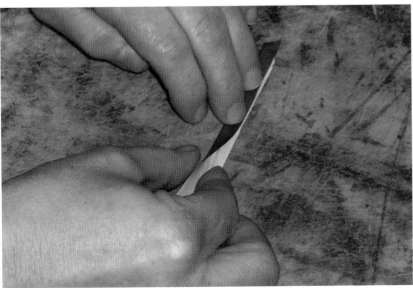

Run a strip of ¼" double-sided tape down one edge of the beading strip. *Do not* put the double-sided tape right on the edge of the beading; position it about ⅛" from the edge.

Pull the paper off the tape. Fold the leather strip in half over a cord to create beading. When folding, line up the top leather edge with the tape edge, *not* the bottom leather edge. Tip: Hold the cord taut and work in small sections—½" at a time.

Apply another strip of double-sided tape to the completed beading strip. Position it right next to the rounded cord. Fold the beading strip in half to find the middle. Position the bracelet in the center and carefully mark *exactly* each corner. Cut a triangle out at each mark that extends right up to the enclosed cord.

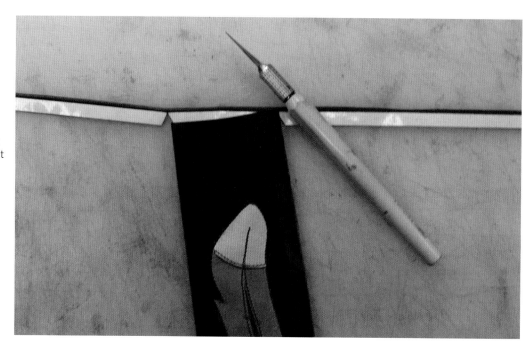

Fold the beading strip at the cut-out triangles to create a corner. If the cut-out triangles were positioned correctly the beading should exactly fit around the bracelet.

Lay the bracelet on the beading between the corners, then apply the beading down each side. The best technique is to leave the beading strip laying flat and bring the bracelet down to the beading a little at a time. Try to leave only the corded area of the beading visible.

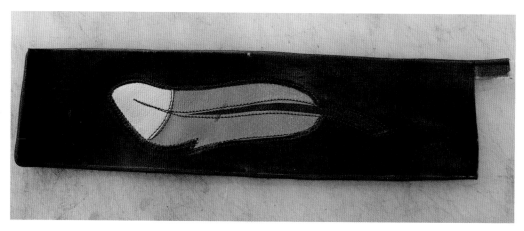

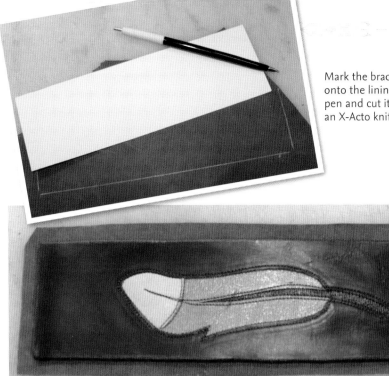

Mark the bracelet lining pattern onto the lining leather with a silver pen and cut it out with scissors or an X-Acto knife.

Apply Aquilim GL to the back of the bracelet and then lay it onto the bracelet lining. Lightly tap the bracelet and lining together, allow the glue to dry for a few minutes, and stitch around all four edges.

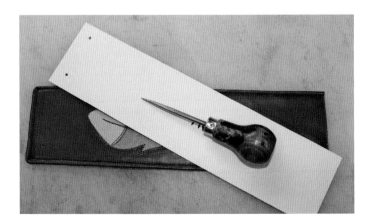

After stitching, trim the excess lining with an edger, seam ripper, or small sharp scissors.

Using the bracelet pattern, mark where the snaps should be positioned. Use an awl to make the marks on the top side of the bracelet at one end and on the lining side of the bracelet at the other end. The awl marks show where to position and place the snaps.

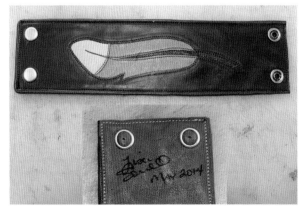

Place the snaps at both ends of the finished bracelet and don't forget to sign and date it on the back!

Lisa Sorrell is a master cowboy boot maker and leather artist. She has won multiple awards for her work in the United States and internationally. Sorrell is a featured artist on the PBS series *Craft in America* and her work has been featured in numerous books. The owner of Sorrell Custom Boots, she speaks, writes, and teaches on both cowboy boot making and the decorative art of leather inlay and overlay. She lives in Oklahoma.

www.sorrellnotionsandfindings.com

On "It's a Boot Life," Sorrell demonstrates both boot making and leather working techniques: www.youtube.com/customboots

Photo by Sarah Willson